D0770789

Czech History

Czech History

Kytka Hilmarová

CZECH REVIVAL
PUBLISHING

Czech History. Copyright © 2023 by Kytka Hilmarová

All rights reserved. No part of this publication may be reproduced, distributed, or transmitted in any form or by any means, including photocopying, recording, or other electronic or mechanical methods, without the prior written permission of the publisher, except in the case of brief quotations embodied in critical reviews and specific other noncommercial uses permitted by copyright law. For permission requests or information about special discounts or bulk purchases, please contact:

Czech Revival Publishing.
www.czechrevival.com
US+ 727-238-7884

The views expressed in this work are the author's own and may not reflect the opinions or policies of any organization or individual. The author's personal experiences and opinions are shared for entertainment and educational purposes. Readers are encouraged to form their own conclusions based on the content presented. The author assumes no responsibility for the reader's actions. References to people, organizations, or events are based on the author's translation, recollection, and/or interpretation. This work does not provide professional advice, and readers should consult experts in relevant fields for guidance.

Library of Congress Cataloging-in-Publication Data

Hilmarova, Kytka 1964-
       Czech History / Kytka Hilmarová

Summary: "Czech History" by Kytka Hilmarova is a captivating exploration of the Czech nation's past, encompassing centuries of triumphs, struggles, and cultural achievements. With meticulous research and a passion for storytelling, Hilmarova invites readers on a journey through time, from the ancient roots of the Slavic tribes to the vibrant cultural renaissance, the challenges of independence, and the complexities of the modern era. With its comprehensive and engaging narrative, this book celebrates the remarkable individuals who have shaped Czech history and offers a deeper understanding and appreciation of the nation's rich heritage.

ISBN-13: 978-1-943103-30-0

1. History / Europe / Eastern 2. Biography & Autobiography / Historical 3. Social Science / Ethnic Studies / European 4. Hilmarova, Kytka.

To my beloved parents, Anna and Milan Hilmar, I express my heartfelt gratitude for instilling in me the unwavering sense of pride in my Czech heritage. No matter where I have resided, you have reminded me that I am and will always be a proud Czech at heart.

To my dear children, Zynnia, Zanna, and Zachary, I impart upon you the importance of embracing your roots with unwavering pride. May you always carry the knowledge of our Czech heritage with a sense of honor, just as I do when I look upon each of you.

And to all my cherished readers, I invite you to embark on a profound journey through the rich tapestry of our Czech heritage. May the spirit of Bohemia guide you, illuminating the path as you explore the resilience, beauty, and profound spirit that permeates our nation's history. May this journey inspire within you a deep appreciation for our remarkable heritage and leave you with a profound sense of connection and pride.

Table of Contents

Foreword

In the pages that follow, you will embark on a journey through the rich tapestry of Czech history. This book, titled "Czech History," stands as a tribute to the past and a celebration of the remarkable individuals who have shaped the course of our nation.

However, it is important to acknowledge the origins of this work. While its foundation lies in the writings of Josef Václav Nikolau, a talented author who accomplished much in his tragically short life, it has undergone significant transformation. What began as a translation of his work, "Dějepis český v obrazích pro českoslovanskou mládež na Skolílch národních," has evolved into a comprehensive reinterpretation, combining elements from the original text with substantial additions and reimagined prose.

The intention behind this endeavor was to bring Czech history to life for contemporary readers, addressing the linguistic challenges presented by the book's 19th-century Czech language and incorporating a more inclusive and engaging narrative. While preserving the essence of Nikolau's vision, "Czech History" by Kytka Hilmarova encompasses a wider scope, presenting events and perspectives that have shaped our nation since the 1870s.

In the spirit of honoring the author's legacy, it is important to recognize the invaluable groundwork laid by Josef Václav Nikolau. His original work provided the inspiration and structure for this endeavor, serving as a guiding light for the expansion and exploration of Czech history that follows.

Additionally, this revised edition includes a detailed chronology, serving as a valuable companion to the narrative. It offers a timeline of significant events, allowing readers to contextualize the historical developments that unfold within these pages.

Now, let us begin this captivating journey through Czech history. Together, we will uncover the triumphs, struggles, and extraordinary stories that have shaped our nation. May this book serve as an invitation to delve into the past, fostering a deeper understanding and appreciation of our shared heritage.

Introduction

The beautiful Czech land, emerges at the heart of Europe, encircled by majestic mountains. Only towards the east and southeast can we, as travelers, venture into Moravia or Austria (Lower Austria) without the rugged terrain reminding us of the mountainous journey. Its shape resembles an irregular quadrilateral, with its four corners pointing towards the cardinal directions. The mountain ranges along its borders are adorned with lush forests that transition into enchanting groves and delightful landscapes within the country. Countless springs, streams, and rivers, both small and mighty, meander through valleys like shimmering ribbons, converging within the land to form the magnificent river, the Elbe, which flows out through a single gorge to the north. Nestled among these valleys, amidst branching trees, one can find tranquil villages, ancient castles, and thriving cities—the abodes of the singing, cheerful Czech people. It is within this blessed land that our parents, friends, siblings, teachers, and educators all reside—each and every one of them.

These are the very lands that have nurtured us, where our predecessors lived before us. Our fathers, grandfathers, and great-grandfathers called this place home, and they were esteemed for their warmth, integrity, joyful spirits, and indomitable courage. Many coveted these blessed lands, hoping to claim them for themselves. Yet, the Czechs welcomed them with open hearts, valiantly defending the land passed down to them by their beloved ancestors. They would have willingly sacrificed their lives rather than let their homeland fall into the hands of foreigners. Such was their profound love for it! And we, too, passionately adore our beautiful homeland, for it offers countless reasons to cherish it. It overflows with abundant gifts, harboring immense prosperity that makes it one of the most delightful and thriving nations in the world. Moreover, it boasts a glorious past, a tapestry woven with rich history.

Have you ever gazed into a mirror and realized that you see yourself reflected in it? History, or historiography, is akin to a mirror, although slightly different. It does not reflect us or our immediate ancestors, but rather, it acquaints us with the remarkable deeds of our forefathers. It reveals how they shaped the land many years ago, how they contributed to its prosperity and enrichment, and so much more. By delving into this understanding, we can express our gratitude and beseech the Creator, God, to bestow abundant blessings upon our ancestors for their dedicated care towards us.

Every garden, every grove within our homeland exudes bliss, and our hearts rejoice as we behold its beauty. In this land, we find our own paradise, a place that holds our dreams, memories, and hopes for the future.

Ancient Bohemia

In our beloved homeland, things were not always as peaceful as they are today. In the early days, the entire land was covered by water, resembling a vast sea. However, a transformative event occurred when God commanded, "Let the waters under the heavens be gathered together into one place, and let dry land appear." As a result, three islands emerged within our land: one large island encompassing the western and southern regions of Bohemia, and two smaller ones in the northeast. The rest of the land remained submerged beneath the sea. These islands, though, were barren and lifeless. Not a single blade of grass or creature could be found. Additionally, an intense heat prevailed, attributed to the presence of scorching liquids deep within our land.

This era is known as the period of primordial hills. The period of primordial hills, also referred to as the Paleozoic Era, encompasses a vast expanse of geological time from approximately 541 to 252 million years ago. During this era, Earth experienced remarkable changes, with the emergence and evolution of diverse life forms in ancient oceans, the formation of majestic mountain ranges, and the development of the Earth's first landmasses. It was a dynamic period that laid the foundation for the subsequent evolution of life and the shaping of our planet's landscapes.

However, mighty rivers flowed from these islands into the surrounding sea, carrying with them an abundance of mud, sand, and stones from the land's interior. Over time, this accumulation rose above the water, forming solid ground. Even then, the land remained desolate. This phase is referred to as a transitional period.

Within the muddy lowlands of the solid land, peculiar plants resembling today's ferns and horsetails thrived, but they grew to the size of trees. The vegetation was undoubtedly abundant. As the sands and mud settled, they gradually transformed into the coal that our land is renowned for, surpassing many other regions. Simultaneously, salt began to accumulate in the seabed surrounding Bohemia, causing our land to rise significantly above sea level and resulting in its scarcity of salt. However, the sea once again intruded into Bohemia, depositing layers of sandstone and limestone on its seabed, leading to the demise of numerous marine creatures.

This period is known as the era of the Cretaceous Sea. During the era of the Cretaceous Sea, which spanned from approximately 145 to 66 million years ago, vast portions of the Earth's surface were covered by a shallow sea. This period witnessed significant geological and biological transformations, including the dominance of dinosaurs, the emergence of new marine life forms, and the formation of iconic geological features that continue to shape our planet's landscape.

Throughout time, Bohemia underwent various tumultuous transformations, such as the eruption of fiery substances through these layers or shifts in different directions. Consequently, the present state of our homeland gradually took shape. However, during that time, the climate was still as warm as it is in North Africa, where the black people reside. Walnut trees, maples, beeches, and even some palms thrived abundantly. In their shade, herds of mammals grazed, including majestic elephants and bathing rhinoceroses in our rivers. Additionally, warm springs like those found in Teplice and Karlovy Vary emerged during this period.

Only then did a period of tranquility ensue, and the land became ready to welcome human generations. Oaks, beeches, and maples thrived, while spruces, firs, and pines adorned the lofty mountains. Our forests became home to herds of elk, bears, and European bison—they reigned supreme. Finally, humans arrived, becoming the masters of this world. Forests yielded to their axes, and wild animals made way for their cultivated fields.

Regarding the first settlement of humans in Bohemia, their origins, and the tribes they belonged to, much remains unknown. Speculations suggest that the land was initially inhabited by people of various ethnic backgrounds, including individuals of Nordic heritage and individuals of East Asian heritage. These non-warlike individuals existed at a primitive stage of civilization. Metals remained undiscovered, and their tools were fashioned from wood and stone. Along the rivers, they built simple huts, clearing the forests to a degree comparable to certain indigenous tribes in America. To fell a tree, they would hollow out a hole in the trunk using a stone tool, place burning coal within, and then use a stone mallet to bring down the charred trunk.

In time, these tribes were likely conquered by other Indo-European peoples. It is possible that several tribes from this lineage inhabited Bohemia, but specific details regarding their identities and characteristics remain unknown. Further research and ongoing archaeological discoveries continue to provide valuable insights into the ancient inhabitants of Bohemia, deepening our understanding of their cultures, customs, and civilizations. Through the study of artifacts, burial sites, and ancient settlements, historians and archaeologists are uncovering new information about the diverse societies that once thrived in the region. This ongoing exploration of Bohemia's past enables us to piece together a more comprehensive picture of the rich history and heritage of this remarkable land. The story of our homeland's early human settlement is a fascinating puzzle that continues to intrigue scholars and historians.

As we explore the rich history of our land, we uncover a tapestry of events and civilizations that have shaped its identity. From the primordial hills to the emergence of mighty rivers, the formation of coal deposits, and the diverse flora and fauna that once thrived here, our homeland has endured countless transformations throughout the ages.

In the upcoming chapters, we will embark on an immersive journey into the captivating history of Bohemia. We will trace the footsteps of our ancestors, exploring the dynamic narratives of ancient kingdoms, and unearthing the cultural, social, and political milestones that have shaped our cherished homeland into the vibrant nation it stands as today. From the earliest human settlements to the medieval era, the Renaissance, and beyond, we will delve into the depths of time, unraveling the remarkable stories of the Czech people and their enduring contributions to the world. Join us as we uncover the rich tapestry of Bohemia's past and celebrate the legacy of a resilient and visionary nation.

How the Boii Came to Bohemia

If we were to venture westward, far beyond the vast forests and thriving mines, our path would lead us to the land we now know as France. But in ancient times, this land was known as Gaul, home to the Gauls or Celts, a proud and resilient people. Among their kings was a ruler named Ambigatus, who was beloved by his subjects for his kindness, justice, and deep affection for his people. Yet, despite the richness of the land, there was a prevailing challenge that weighed heavily on King Ambigatus' heart - the struggles of his people due to poverty and scarcity. The population had grown, and the resources of Gaul could no longer sustain everyone's needs.

In response to this pressing concern, King Ambigatus turned to his two nephews, Bellovesus and Sigovesus, two courageous and determined young men. He entrusted them with a mission, saying, "Gather a multitude of people and seek out new lands where you can thrive without being overwhelmed by outsiders." Moved by their uncle's plea, Bellovesus and Sigovesus embarked on their journey, bidding farewell to their beloved homeland. Sigovesus led his people across the mighty Rhine River, venturing into the Hercynian forests that stretched east of the Rhine. It was through their relentless pursuit that they finally arrived in a land that would become our cherished homeland, Bohemia. The Boii, as they came to be known, settled not only in Bohemia but also in Moravia and the two archduchies of Austria. They established their roots and built a new community, bringing with them their customs, traditions, and aspirations.

Bohemia, or Boiohaemum as it was called, became a land of promise and opportunity, shaped by the resilience and determination of those who sought a better future. It was a land where the Boii thrived, coexisting with the enchanting landscapes, nurturing the bonds of community, and forging their own unique identity. From that moment on, the Boii and their descendants, the Czech people, have woven their stories into the tapestry of Bohemian history, leaving an indelible mark on the land they now call home.

The Fate of the Boii

During those times, the Boii were known for their knowledge and sophistication. They established permanent settlements, residing in cottages, villages, and even fortified cities. Their way of life encompassed various roles - warriors, hunters, shepherds, and farmers - as they navigated the challenges of their environment. They were resilient, relying on war plunder, agriculture, livestock breeding, craftsmanship, and trade to sustain themselves. Skilled artisans, they crafted exquisite vessels using copper and iron. Clad in leather attire, they exuded cheerfulness and practiced frugality in their daily lives.

While the Boii were not aggressors, they displayed unwavering bravery when their land faced invasion. However, there came a moment of great adversity. Around 48 years before the birth of Christ, Berebista, the powerful Dacian king who ruled over Transdanubian Hungary and Sibinsko, launched an attack against them. A fierce battle ensued, resulting in the Boii's devastating defeat and the destruction of their land along the Danube, which is now known as present-day Austria. Since then, it has been remembered as the "Boii wasteland."

The Boii, regrettably, never fully recovered from this profound setback. In later years, the Marcomanni arrived, and they either subjected, exterminated, or displaced the Boii from their ancestral settlements, leaving a lasting impact on their once-thriving communities.

Maroboduus, the King of the Markomanni

During the first century BC, the Markomanni, a Germanic people who spoke the Germanic language, resided alongside their relatives and allies, the Quadi, in the vicinity of the middle Odra River. As the Boii tribe weakened, the Markomanni migrated southward, traversing Moravia until they reached the Danube River, ultimately settling in the heart of what is now present-day Hungary. It was in this region that they found themselves in close proximity to the Romans, who at the time held the distinction of being the most powerful nation. The Romans had already achieved conquests in Italy and expanded their dominion to encompass lands spanning the Mediterranean Sea in Europe, Asia, and Africa.

Maroboduus, hailing from a noble aristocratic family, spent his formative years in Rome, where he acquired expertise in the art of warfare and garnered knowledge across various disciplines. Upon returning to his homeland, he ascended to a position of leadership, establishing a royal court and forging a formidable empire. His realm encompassed the present-day territories of Bohemia, Moravia, and Slovakia. Recognizing the threat posed by the mighty Romans, numerous other Germanic tribes rallied under Maroboduus's banner, seeking his leadership and protection in defense against the powerful Roman forces. As a testament to his influence, Maroboduus chose to make his residence in the former capital of the Boii tribe, which was subsequently named Marobudum in his honor.

During that era, the Markomanni, much like other Germanic tribes of the time, were known for their rugged nature and nomadic lifestyle, as they did not establish permanent settlements. Their dwellings consisted of scattered huts situated near springs and streams, while some sought shelter in pits and caves during the harsh winter months. Within their society, a hierarchical division existed, separating the nobles or freemen from the serfs.

The nobles primarily engaged in acts of warfare and hunting, delegating other tasks to the serfs. Their sustenance relied heavily on a diet of meat, milk, cheese, and occasional consumption of raw or cooked game. Their attire lacked intricate craftsmanship, and they primarily relied on fur and leather for clothing and protection. Their religious beliefs leaned towards paganism, and it was not uncommon for them to offer human sacrifices to their gods. Despite these practices, they held high regard for moral purity, modesty, and hospitality, which were considered admirable qualities within their society.

Maroboduus gained immense fame, to the point where even the Roman Emperor Augustus grew fearful of him. This led the Romans to dispatch two armies in an attempt to conquer him. However, their plans faced a sudden twist when the Pannonian and Dalmatian tribes rebelled against Rome, diverting the Romans' attention towards quelling the rebellion. In a strategic move, the Romans formed an alliance with Maroboduus to join forces against the rebels. However, this arrangement did not sit well with the Germans, who harbored animosity towards the Romans.

Three years later, a young Cheruscan prince named Arminius, also known as Herman, emerged as a heroic figure. He repaid the Germans' discontent by orchestrating a stunning victory over a formidable Roman army led by Varus. This triumph took place deep within Germanic territory, specifically in the Teutoburg Forest, resulting in the liberation of oppressed Germanic tribes. Maroboduus, however, disapproved of Herman's tactics, which fueled the resentment among the Germans.

In the year 17 AD, a significant war erupted between Maroboduus and Herman, marking a memorable chapter in their history. The battle unfolded in the Saxony region, displaying the strength and determination of both sides. Although the outcome remained indecisive, a pivotal moment occurred when Maroboduus attempted to retreat to a nearby hill. To his dismay, his own troops betrayed him, defecting to join Herman's forces. In the face of this betrayal, Maroboduus was compelled to retreat to Bohemia, seeking refuge from the tumultuous events unfolding around him.

In a twist of fate, two years later, Katvald, a prince of the Goths and a Germanic tribe whom Maroboduus had previously expelled from his land, launched an invasion into Bohemia. This opportunistic attack resulted in the seizure of Maroboduus's seat of power, along with all his cherished treasures, in the year 19 AD.

Left abandoned by those who once stood by him, Maroboduus sought refuge with his cunning friends, the Romans. Emperor Tiberius, in an act of generosity, granted him residence in the city of Ravenna. For the next eighteen years, Maroboduus lived under Roman protection, sheltered from the adversities that had befallen him. Meanwhile, the Markomanni, weakened by internal conflicts and disputes, entered a long period of weakness. Their infighting took a toll on the land of Bohemia, leaving it desolate and bereft of its people.

A timeless Czech proverb reminds us that "pride goes before a fall." The proud Maroboduus, once revered and powerful, experienced the consequences of his hubris. Let us all take heed and be cautious of pride, akin to a venomous snake. Instead, let humility guide us, for it is through humility that we find favor with God.

During the reign of Maroboduus, an important figure in the history of the Marcomanni tribe, a significant event unfolded in a distant corner of the world—the birth of Jesus Christ. While Maroboduus focused on consolidating his power and expanding the influence of the Marcomanni, a profound religious and cultural transformation was taking place in the region of Judea, where the birth of Jesus marked the beginning of a new era. This event, though seemingly unrelated to Maroboduus and his endeavors, would go on to shape the course of human history in profound ways. The teachings and actions of Jesus would eventually spread throughout the Roman Empire, influencing the lives and beliefs of countless individuals across different cultures and civilizations. It serves as a reminder that while rulers and kingdoms pursued their ambitions and conflicts on a geopolitical stage, the world at large continued to evolve, driven by spiritual and ideological forces that transcended territorial boundaries.

The Marcomannic War

In the 2nd century AD, the tribes residing in the regions traversed by the mighty rivers Odra and Vistula grew restless and embarked on raids against their southern neighbors, which included the formidable Roman Empire.

The audacity of these tribal incursions sparked great concern among the Romans, especially the renowned emperor Marcus Aurelius, instilling fear throughout the empire. Recognizing the gravity of the situation, the emperor made a decisive move by liquidating the treasury to ensure the soldiers' wages were paid. Meanwhile, every Roman citizen rallied together, contributing their utmost to support the war effort. The combined efforts culminated in the formation of a formidable army that set out to confront the relentless adversaries.

The ensuing conflict, known as the Marcomannic War, waged on for a grueling span of fifteen years, exacting a heavy toll on both sides. The battlefields were drenched in blood as the Roman forces clashed fiercely against their determined foes.

This momentous conflict left an indelible mark on history, forever etching the name Marcomannic War into the annals of the Roman Empire.

The emperor himself found himself compelled to take the field multiple times to confront the relentless enemies. In one particular invasion of the Quadian land, which corresponds to present-day Slovakia, the Roman army encountered a parched and waterless region. The scorching heat and unyielding thirst afflicted both soldiers and horses. To exacerbate matters, the adversaries emerged on the hills, poised for an imminent attack. Facing certain doom, the soldiers were tempted to discard their weapons and flee from the imminent danger.

However, as the saying goes, in moments of utmost desperation, divine intervention often makes its presence known. In a remarkable turn of events, a magnificent storm materialized seemingly out of nowhere, casting a striking spectacle of lightning and thunderbolts that pierced through the air. As if a gift from the heavens, torrential rain poured down upon the weary army, quenching their thirst and revitalizing their weary souls. Seizing this unexpected blessing, the soldiers eagerly raised their helmets, catching every precious drop of the life-giving water. Filled with newfound strength and courage, they charged forth with unwavering determination, launching an assault of unrivaled ferocity against their adversaries.

Simultaneously, a powerful gust of wind surged forward, propelling the rain directly into the faces of the enemy, causing them great difficulty in their advance. This unforeseen obstacle worked to the advantage of the Romans, contributing to their resounding victory—a triumph that surpassed all expectations given the seemingly insurmountable odds they had encountered. It was undoubtedly a miraculous deliverance, a testament to their unyielding determination and the fortuitous intervention of nature itself. Emerging from this extraordinary episode, the Romans emerged victorious, their fate forever altered by the timely assistance and twist of fortune bestowed upon them by the very forces of nature.

According to ancient chronicles, it is recounted that among the ranks of the mighty Roman army stood soldiers who professed the Christian faith. In their darkest hour of distress, these devout individuals humbly knelt in prayer, beseeching for divine intervention and solace. Miraculously, their earnest supplications were answered, as rain descended from the heavens in a response to their unwavering faith. This extraordinary turn of events left an indelible impression on the Roman soldiers, leading them to bestow upon this particular unit the moniker of the "Lightning Legion." This remarkable occurrence, steeped in faith and divine intervention, transpired in the year 174 AD, forever etching its memory in the annals of history.

However, even with the intervention of nature and the miraculous events that unfolded, the war continued to rage on, persisting until the final days of Emperor Marcus Aurelius. It was in the city of Vindobona, known today as Vienna, where the emperor breathed his last breath in the year 180 AD. With his passing, a significant chapter in history came to an end, signifying the culmination of a tumultuous and protracted conflict that had plagued the Roman Empire for an extended period of time. The emperor's demise marked a turning point, bringing closure to a chapter filled with struggle and shaping the course of the empire's future.

Slavs

In ancient times, believed to be around 1500 years before the birth of Christ, our ancestors, the Slavs, thrived in significant numbers throughout Eastern Europe. These peaceful and industrious people embraced a lifestyle centered around settled communities, engaging in agriculture, craftsmanship, and trade. Wars were a last resort for them, primarily reserved for self-defense. Their humble abodes consisted of simple cottages constructed from hewn wood, often nestled amidst the tranquility of forests, in remote and inaccessible areas close to rivers, lakes, and marshes.

Characterized by their diminutive stature, the Slavs possessed sturdy limbs, round faces, captivating dark blue eyes, and brownish hair. They exhibited remarkable resilience in the face of hunger, thirst, cold, and heat, bearing these challenges with unwavering patience. The Slavs took immense pride in their work, with farming and gardening standing as their preferred occupations. They were trailblazers in the realm of agriculture, skillfully reaping the bountiful harvests from their fields. Flour-based meals were a particular favorite among them, and in addition to water, they savored the flavors of mead and beer, which graced their communal gatherings.

The Slavs, with their gentle and peace-loving nature, embodied diligence and kindness. Hospitality was their virtue, as they warmly welcomed anyone who crossed their path. Even in times of conflict, they treated captives and strangers with respect, often granting captives the opportunity to integrate into Slavic society or return safely after a designated period. Among their many passions, the Slavs held a deep love for singing, music, and dancing. However, their lack of unity often led to internal discord, resulting in misfortunes befalling their communities. The Germans and Sarmatians, being more adept in warfare than the Slavs, seized the opportunity to subjugate them.

Preferring the tranquility of a peaceful existence, the Slavs did not prioritize training in the arts of warfare. They held a disdain for arms and conflicts, opting instead to endure injustices rather than perpetrate them. The desire for power over others was foreign to them, as they embraced a society without rulers above themselves. In this egalitarian system, all citizens enjoyed equal freedom, rights, and responsibilities. The land was divided into communal communities, encompassing mountains, forests, pastures, lakes, and rivers, accessible for all to utilize according to their needs. Villages, on the other hand, consisted of fields and gardens, privately owned and passed down from fathers to sons as a hereditary legacy.

The Slavic people of ancient times adhered to a pagan religion, engaging in rituals that involved the creation of idols fashioned from various metals and the construction of temples dedicated to their worship. These practices formed an integral part of their spiritual lives. In addition to their idolatrous customs, the Slavs held beliefs in the immortality of the soul and the notion of fair retribution in the afterlife. These beliefs shaped their understanding of the spiritual realm and provided them with a moral framework that governed their actions in the earthly realm.

The Slavic people were characterized by their genuine care and concern for one another, constantly offering well-wishes and finding joy in the accomplishments of their fellow members. Their deep-rooted commitment to peaceful coexistence serves as an inspiring example of harmonious living. As individuals fortunate enough to be part of the Slavic community, we can take great pride in our association with such a remarkable tribe. This legacy of unity and empathy continues to shape our collective identity and reminds us of the importance of fostering compassion and goodwill in our interactions with one another.

With a population exceeding 50 million individuals, the vibrant and diverse Slavic community encompasses four prominent branches: Czech-Slovaks, Poles, Russians, and South Slavs. The very name "Slav" carries a profound significance, often associated with the word "slava" meaning "glory." This connection reflects our ancestors' deep appreciation for achieving greatness and their remarkable accomplishments that have brought honor to our shared heritage. As members of the Slavic community, we inherit this legacy of resilience, cultural richness, and a collective pursuit of glory that continues to shape our present and inspire our future.

Czech-Slovaks

The ancient peoples held a different attachment to their dwellings compared to our present mindset. If they were dissatisfied with their current land, they would embark on migrations to seek new territories.

In the 5th century, a group of our forefathers, the Slavs, undertook a migration from east to west. Their leader, Czech, guided them through mountains and valleys, venturing from the vast region known as Charvátsko or Bělocharvátsko on the northern side of the Carpathian Mountains. They traversed far and wide, bounded by three rivers, until they arrived in our cherished homeland. Upon reaching Mount Ripa, situated between the Elbe, Vltava, and Ohře rivers, they halted their journey. Czech himself ascended the mountain, surveying the surrounding landscape to assess its fertility. Witnessing an abundance of forests teeming with game and birds, rich sources of honey and milk, and the magnificent adornment of mountains, he addressed his fellow countrymen with heartfelt words:

"Brothers! Together, we have endured immense toil and overcome countless hardships, navigating through impassable forests. Let us take a moment to offer a rare sacrifice to our gods, whose aid has finally brought us to this marvelous land, predestined for us by fate. This land, as I have often promised, is harmless to anyone, brimming with game, birds, honey, and milk. Moreover, its favorable climate makes it exceptionally suitable for habitation. Waters flow abundantly from all directions, and the presence of numerous fishponds further adds to its allure. You shall have an abundance of all these blessings, for no harm shall befall you. Now, contemplate the joyous responsibility that lies in our hands. Together, let us decide upon a name befitting this land."

"Hail, our father Czech!" echoed Czech's loyal retinue. "Let us name it Czechy! Czechy, Czechy, so shall it be!"

And thus, our homeland came to be known as Czechy, carrying the legacy of our revered leader Czech.

Overwhelmed with joy, Czech embraced the earth, planting a kiss upon its surface, before rising to his feet and raising his hands towards the heavens. With profound gratitude, he proclaimed, "Welcome, land that was destined for us, attained through countless promises we fervently beseeched. May you preserve our well-being and may our descendants multiply from generation to generation!"

And so, the inaugural offering was kindled on the Czech land, a solemn tribute dedicated to the Slavic deities. Czech's retinue descended from the mountain and established their first settlement at the foot of this sacred place. The fertile soil was marked by the furrows of the Slavic plow, as they began their diligent work.

According to our national tradition, Czech himself chose to settle in the city of Ctěnice, nestled beneath a prominent hill. It is said that upon his passing, Czech was laid to rest beneath a grand mound, forever enshrined within the embrace of his beloved land.

Our ancestors, driven by their diverse branches, established settlements that suited their respective regions. Along the left bank of the Elbe, spanning the Vltava and Berounka rivers, the main branch settled, forming the heart of what we now know as Čechy (Bohemia). To the east of them, the Zličans found their home, while the Lučans settled on both sides of the Ohře River to the northwest. The Sedličans made their abode in the present-day Litoměřice region, extending their reach to the west. Towards the south, the Pšovans established their territory, while the Charváts thrived above the upper Jizera River. And in the areas we now recognize as Budějovice and Písek, the vibrant community of the Dúdlebovs flourished.

It is worth noting that while the Czechs embarked on their journey, other Slavic brethren from the same Bělocharvátsko region embarked on their own migrations. These kindred souls settled beyond the Morava River in Moravia, expanding their presence to lands above the Váh, Nitra, and Hron rivers in present-day Hungary, predominantly to the south and extending as far as the Danube. The colonization of our current Czech-Slavic territories did not occur instantaneously but unfolded gradually between the years 451 and approximately 500 AD, with a temporal gap of around fifty years.

Our esteemed ancestors were primarily engaged in the noble pursuit of agriculture, embarking on the ambitious task of clearing forests and draining marshlands to create fertile grounds for their villages and towns. Their diligent efforts yielded abundant agricultural produce, allowing them to extend their generosity to their neighbors by providing grains and livestock in exchange for essential commodities like salt and other necessities. Not only were they skilled in the art of farming, but they also possessed remarkable craftsmanship and traded their exquisite creations made from iron, bronze, and silver.

Furthermore, their unity and love for one another were akin to the unconditional affection between parents and their cherished children, as well as the profound respect that worthy offspring hold for their parents. The head of each family assumed the role of a patriarch, and upon his passing, a chosen elder would step forward to carry the torch of responsibility. This esteemed elder skillfully managed the household affairs, skillfully delegating tasks among the children and servants. Referred to as a zeman, this individual held ownership of a piece of land, often an entire village. Those zemen who possessed larger portions of land were bestowed the title of lech, signifying their noble stature. Among these noble figures, those who held religious offices were known as priests or princes. It was customary for these princes, nobles, and elders to convene periodically at assemblies, where they would consult with one another on strategic measures to safeguard their lands against potential threats and enemies.

The Czechs thrived in an atmosphere of fraternal love, finding contentment and joy in their harmonious existence. Their thoughts were sincere and filled with goodwill towards one another, always ready to lend a helping hand in times of adversity, never causing harm. It was a land where they flourished, finding true fulfillment.

Let us rejoice, fellow Czechs, for we are fortunate inhabitants of this abundant and fertile land, guided by divine providence. Within its borders, a veritable treasure trove awaits us, offering an abundance of grains, fruits, livestock, birds, and valuable resources such as metals and coal. Our beloved homeland has been graciously bestowed upon us by the benevolence of a higher power, and it is our noble responsibility to enrich its prosperity and reputation through our honorable endeavors. As true Czechs, let us embrace our language, our nation, and this cherished land with profound love, upholding the legacy of our ancestors by preserving their timeless customs and rights. Together, let us forge a future that honors their enduring spirit and secures the enduring greatness of our homeland.

Samo, The First Slavic King

The path of the Czechs was not always smooth and prosperous. In approximately 558 AD, a formidable horde known as the Avars emerged from Asia and made their way into Europe. They settled in the land of Hungary and soon began launching devastating raids into neighboring territories, including the Czech lands in 563 AD. Our beloved ancestors fell under their oppressive rule, enduring the plundering of their resources and the loss of countless lives to those who dared to resist. The Czechs made valiant attempts to break free from their grip, but it wasn't until 622 AD that their fortunes began to change.

Enter Samo, a Slavic warrior whose origins can be traced to the Slavic lands of the Wends, located in present-day Netherlands. Possessing remarkable courage and battle-tested experience, Samo became a beacon of hope for the Czechs. They rallied behind him, and in 623 AD, they launched a powerful revolt against the Avars, emerging victorious and reclaiming their lands. The Avars, in the face of the Czechs' determined resistance, dared not return. Europe breathed a sigh of relief as the wild horde that had struck fear across the continent was expelled by the Czechs and Moravians.

In a display of deep gratitude, the Czechs and Moravians elected Samo as their king around 627 AD. With his rule extending from the eastern Tatra Mountains to the western Šumava Mountains, and from the southern Sprewa and Havel rivers to the majestic Krkonoše Mountains, Samo became the first Slavic ruler in Bohemia. His seat of power was in Vyšehrad, where he governed with wisdom and justice for an impressive 35 years. The Czechs held Samo dear in their hearts, forever grateful for his leadership and the liberation he had brought.

However, Dagobert, the king of the Franks, couldn't help but covet the success of the Czechs and yearned to exert his rule over them. He deliberated on ways to justify declaring war and subjugating them. In due course, he dispatched his envoy, Sichar, to the Czechs, demanding compensation from Samo for alleged damages caused by his subjects to Frankish merchants in 630 AD.

Samo, a fair and just leader, offered to fully indemnify for the damages on the condition that the Franks would reciprocate by reimbursing Slavic merchants for the losses they had endured at the hands of the Franks. Such a proposition was reasonable and equitable, aiming for a harmonious resolution. However, the envoy, Sichar, remained dissatisfied with this response. Instead, he resorted to threats, insults, and unwarranted assertions of Samo's subordination to King Dagobert. Outraged by this affront, Samo swiftly expelled the envoy from his domain, fiercely asserting the autonomy and dignity of the Czechs.

News of this defiance reached Dagobert, compelling him to swiftly amass his army and march into Bohemia with three formidable columns, determined to compel the Czechs into submission. However, the Czechs, resolute under Samo's guidance, wasted no time in confronting Dagobert head-on. A ferocious battle ensued near Tuhošť[1], lasting an arduous three days and three nights. Ultimately, it was the Czechs who emerged triumphant, forcing the Franks into a hasty retreat.

Nevertheless, Dagobert, undeterred, returned the following year in 631 AD, only to meet another fruitless retreat. Recognizing the indomitable spirit and courage of the Czechs, Dagobert came to the realization that his ambitions were futile. As a result, he chose to pursue a path of peace, making amends with the Czechs.

---

[1] Tuhošť, called Tagosf or Tugosta in Old Czech, is present-day Domažlice, which lies before a wide valley in the Czech mountains, where the Germans have historically launched plundering raids into Bohemia.

During this period of peace, the Czechs seized the opportunity to concentrate on cultivating their fields, meadows, and gardens, utilizing the fruits of their labor for their own advancement and prosperity. This exemplified their resilience and determination in the face of external threats, steadfastly preserving their independence and unwavering commitment to self-governance.

Budeček School

After the passing of Samo, the pioneering Slavic empire he had established began to disintegrate. Each nation within the empire once again selected its own princes and chieftains. In Bohemia, a wise and esteemed figure named Krok assumed the role of the nation's judge and priest, presiding from the revered seat of Vyšehrad.

In those ancient times, the Czech-Slavic people did not possess the level of education they enjoy today. The ability to read and write was unknown to them, as formal schools were nonexistent, and no one had taken up the task of teaching them. Recognizing the need for education among his people, Krok made a momentous decision to establish a school for the Czechs. And true to his resolve, he set forth to bring his vision to fruition. The location chosen for this endeavor was Budče, which remains the oldest school in Bohemia. The precise whereabouts of Budeč have become uncertain over time, with only remnants of old walls, ramparts, and moats visible near the Zákolanský Stream, between the city of Slaný and

Říp Hill. It is believed that a princely castle once stood there, its existence eventually erased by the passage of time, and it was within those walls that the school was situated. However, this was not a school resembling the institutions familiar to us today.

Within those walls, you would not find desks, cabinets, pictures, or maps adorning the space. Instead, you would encounter a handful of roughly hewn stools, idols, herbs, and similar artifacts. At the center of the room stood the master, imparting knowledge to the students on topics such as pagan worship and the wonders of nature. The number of students was modest, as only the affluent nobles could afford to send their sons and daughters there. Nevertheless, these students displayed remarkable diligence and attentiveness, excelling in their studies. Even Krok's three daughters, who possessed exceptional intellect and knowledge, attended this unique school, surpassing their peers from across the Czech lands in their intellectual prowess and wisdom.

Kazi, the eldest of Krok's daughters, possessed extensive knowledge of nature and the healing properties of plants. She dedicated herself to the task of preparing remedies for the sick, using her expertise to provide relief and comfort to those in need.

Teta, on the other hand, devoted her time and efforts to the practice of pagan worship, carrying out the rituals with utmost reverence and piety. Chronicler Cosmas, in his writings, lauded her as someone deserving of praise, for she demonstrated a steadfast commitment to upholding the divine decrees.

The youngest daughter, Libuše, was said to possess a remarkable gift bestowed upon her by the gods - the ability to peer into the future. As an inspired prophetess, she provided insights and foresight that guided the people with her divinely-inspired prophecies.

Not only the daughters but also the sons of the nobles exhibited their own remarkable talents. Přemysl, one of the most accomplished students of Budeček, showcased exceptional aptitude in his studies. Later on, even Saint Wenceslaus, revered for his piety and righteousness, joined the ranks of students at this renowned educational institution. The reputation of Budeček quickly spread throughout Bohemia, attracting students from all corners of the Czech land who sought to acquire knowledge and receive an education in its hallowed halls.

Libuše a Přemysl

When Krok, the revered leader of the Čechs, passed away, the people faced the task of selecting a successor. They turned to Libuše, the daughter of Jebo, a woman of exceptional spirit, noble heart, and remarkable wisdom. Not only was she kind and compassionate, but she also possessed great insight and guidance.

During her reign, Libuše was faced with a challenging dispute between two wealthy brothers over their paternal inheritance. Seeking a fair resolution, she made a decision that the brothers should either rule the estates jointly or divide them equally. However, the elder brother, driven by his desire for complete control, expressed dissatisfaction with the arrangement and began to criticize Libuše. This deeply saddened the princess, leading her to renounce her position as ruler and recommend that the Čech nobles choose a man to serve as their prince.

However, the nobles, recognizing Libuše's wisdom and respecting her leadership, were unwilling to let her step down. They fervently pleaded with her to remain their princess and instead select a Čech man whom they would faithfully obey as their prince.

In response to their plea, Libuše sent a glorious message to the nobleman Přemysl from Stadice[2], a diligent and respected figure whom she knew well from their time together at Budeč school. The messengers arrived at Přemysl's dwelling just as he was concluding his work and preparing to enjoy his humble meal, which consisted of a simple piece of dry bread.

The place where Přemysl received this joyous message is still known today as the "Royal Field." In 1841, Count Ervín of Noetitz erected a stone monument in the center of that ancient field. Adorning the top of the monument was a plow, while the sides featured raised images and an

---

[2] The village of Stadice is indeed located closer to Trmice near the Bělina River in a pleasant valley. However, its inhabitants are no longer direct descendants, including those from whom Přemysl originated. According to legend, one of his distant descendants, King Václav I, felt ashamed as a crowned king to be associated with the common folk of Stadice. He ordered them to be expelled from the village and gave it to the Germans. The memory of Přemysl the Ploughman still persists in that place.)

inscription that read: "Here, Přemysl was called from the plow to the duchy."

Přemysl, known for his gentle and kind nature, ruled as a wise prince, bestowing the land of Bohemia with just and sagacious laws. However, it was his wife who would leave a lasting legacy by establishing the renowned city of Prague, the capital of Bohemia.

On one occasion, Libuše and Přemysl stood alongside the nobles and lords, positioned atop a raised platform on their castle, which afforded them a sweeping view across the forested hills of the Czech land, stretching towards the eastern horizon. It was during this moment that they conceived the idea of constructing a new and formidable castle. As if overcome by a visionary spirit, Libuše exclaimed with unbridled enthusiasm:

"I envision a grand city, its renown reaching the heavens; it shall emerge amidst the forest, its foundations caressed by the flowing waters of the Vltava river."

To the north, the majestic Brusnice (Bruska) stream paints a scenic picture, while to the south, the Petřín hill stands tall, surpassing the surrounding landscape. The very location we stand upon slopes gracefully towards the east, resembling the shape of a dolphin or a sea boar, leading down towards the aforementioned stream and extending all the way to the Vltava river. As you venture towards the stream, you will encounter a man diligently working on a humble threshold amidst the lush forest. This unassuming doorstep commands the respect even of mighty lords. Therefore, let this castle that we shall construct bear the name 'Prague[3]' in honor of this significant site." (Around 723 AD).

Not long after, the nation mourned the passing of Libuše, and her departure was felt deeply by all. It is said that she found her final resting place within the walls of her own castle, Libušín. Přemysl, her beloved husband, soon followed her into eternity, but their legacy continued through their descendants, known as the Přemyslids, who ruled over Bohemia until the 14th century. The Czech people mourned the loss of Přemysl for three solemn days, and he was laid to rest in princely attire at the foot of Vyšehrad, near the gentle stream.

According to an ancient legend, after the passing of Libuše, a group of women led by Vlasta, a

---

[3] Others derive the name Prague from "prah" (Russian "porog"), which means waterfall. It refers to the waterfall created by the Brusnice stream flowing through the Deer Moat beneath Prague Castle, which was founded by Libuše.

former companion of Libuše, conspired to seize control of the land. Allegedly, they either killed or abandoned their husbands and erected a castle known as Děvín, situated near Prague, opposite Vyšehrad. From there, they waged a fierce battle against men. However, their resistance was eventually quelled by the united force of men, resulting in the destruction of the castle of Děvín.

During that era, numerous castles had already emerged across Bohemia, extending beyond the boundaries of Vyšehrad, Prague, Libušín, and Děvín. Within the Křivoklátsko forests, one could find the grand structures of Křivoklát and Krakov. Along the Berounka River, Tětín and Kazín stood with their commanding presence. Tracing the course of the Vltava River, Levý Hradec guarded its shores. In the realm of Lemuzi, the towns of Litoměřice, Bílina, and Děčín flourished. Pšov (now Mělník) arose in the land of Pšovani, while Libice thrived within the land of Zličani. In the western reaches, the city of Plzeň proudly stood, while in the east, Hradec made its mark. These were just a few among many castles and towns that dotted the landscape, each with its own history and significance.

Prince Hostivit

Our beloved homeland, Bohemia, shares its eastern border with the land of Moravia. While Moravia has been a part of Bohemia for many centuries, in ancient times, it had its own rulers and even surpassed Bohemia in power during the 9th century. The wise and just Prince Mojmír reigned over Moravia, earning the love of its people and the fear of neighboring lands. However, his rule did not sit well with Louis, the King of Germany. Fueled by dissatisfaction, Louis amassed a formidable army and invaded Moravia, deposing Mojmír and appointing his nephew Rostislav as the new Moravian prince. With a sense of arrogance, Louis proudly returned through Bohemia to Germany, disregarding any consultation. Such audacity from the German king stirred the anger of the Czech prince of that time, Hostivit, and his courageous Czech warriors.

If Louis held any resentment towards the Czechs before, it only intensified. A fierce war raged between the Germans and the Czechs, lasting for four long years. German armies invaded our homeland, leaving behind a trail of devastation.

Yet, the Czechs refused to surrender. In the face of German mistreatment, they reciprocated with even greater force, returning evil for evil. However, the decisive moment arrived in the year 849 when two mighty armies, the Czechs and the Germans, confronted each other, poised to determine the ultimate victor.

The German forces advanced upon the Czechs with such intensity that the Czechs were compelled to seek refuge in their fortified camp. The losses suffered were significant, leaving the Czechs apprehensive about further battle. To avoid further bloodshed, they dispatched several emissaries to the German camp to negotiate a peace agreement. A truce was seemingly reached. However, in a treacherous turn of events, the Germans exploited the vulnerable state of the Czechs during the negotiations and launched a surprise attack.

Infuriated by this act of treachery, the Czechs swiftly took up arms and fought with unwavering resolve. A fierce and brutal battle ensued. The Czechs fiercely repelled the enemy's assault, inflicting heavy casualties upon their foes. The Germans, realizing the futility of their aggression, retreated to their own camp, only to be pursued by the relentless Czechs. With their defeat inevitable, the Germans were compelled to beg for peace, a peace that carried a heavy price for them. They were required to surrender all their war equipment and weapons to the victorious Czechs, returning home in disgrace.

Thus, after four grueling years of relentless fighting, the war waged by the Czechs under the leadership of the pagan prince Hostivit against Louis the German culminated in a resounding triumph for the Czechs.

Saints Cyril and Methodius

In the coastal region of Macedonia, situated in present-day Turkey, there once thrived an ancient city known as Thessalonike, or Salonika. It was within this historical backdrop that two brothers, Constantine and Methodius, were born during the early 9th century. Their father, Leo, a man of wealth, aspired for his elder son, Methodius, to follow in his footsteps, serving the Byzantine or Greek emperor and the nation as he had done. However, Methodius, already a duke in a Slavic-inhabited region, found no allure in the pursuit of worldly fame and power. Instead, he yearned to dedicate his life to the service of God. Thus, he made the profound decision to enter a monastery nestled on the majestic Mount Olympus.

The younger brother, Constantine, possessed a devout nature even in his youth. Prayer and learning held a special place in his heart, surpassing all other pastimes. Recognizing his remarkable spirit, the guardian of the young princess, Michaela, summoned him to the court, appointing him as a companion to the future ruler of the Greek Empire. As Constantine reached the age of twenty, he was ordained as a priest. It was during this time that the semi-barbaric Khazars, residing in the southern region of Kush near the Black Sea, requested wise Christian teachers from the Greek emperor. Constantine and Methodius were chosen for this task. Placing their trust in God, the brothers embarked on a distant journey, where they successfully converted the prince and prominent figures of that land to the Christian faith. On their return, they carried with them the sacred relics of St. Clement, a former bishop of Rome and the third successor to St. Peter, who had met martyrdom in 102 on the Tauric Peninsula (Crimea).

Shortly after that, Prince Rostislav of Great Moravia made a request to Emperor Michael of Greece for a Christian priest. Constantine and Methodius were chosen for this significant mission, as there were no priests of such caliber available in the Greek Empire. In response to this need, Constantine devised the Slavic alphabet and translated a portion of the Holy Scriptures into the Slavic language. Thus, the holy brothers embarked on their journey to the land of Moravia in the year 863. There, they spread the teachings of Christ among both the rich and the poor, masters and servants. They organized divine services, conducted in the Slavic language, establishing Nitra in Slovakia and Velehrad in Moravia as the centers of their apostolic activities. The people embraced them with open hearts, and their influence led many to the gates of heaven. Day by day, the number of believers grew.

However, as it often happens in this world, even faithful followers of Christ faced adversity. The German bishops, particularly the bishops of Salzburg and Passau, claimed authority over the lands where the two brothers had been tirelessly working. Accused by these bishops, Constantine and Methodius decided to travel to Rome in 867, appointing deputies to carry on their mission in Moravia during their absence.

They continued their preaching to the kind-hearted Slavic people in Hungary, who welcomed them with open arms even on this journey. As they neared Rome, they were greeted by Pope Adrian II, who led a grand procession to meet them. After thoroughly examining their teachings, the Pope not only approved their actions but also sanctioned the use of the Slavic language in divine services. Furthermore, he bestowed upon Methodius the esteemed rank of bishop. Sadly, Saint Cyril's earthly journey came to an end in Rome shortly after, bringing great sorrow to his brother. He passed away on February 14, 869, in a Roman monastery, having taken the name Cyril upon becoming a monk.

Saint Methodius, upon his return to Moravia, made a stop in Kocel, where he and his brother had previously preached. However, as Kocel was under the authority of the German king Louis, he was handed over to the king's men. Methodius endured captivity for a year and a half until, through the powerful intervention of the Pope, he was finally released.

He embarked on another journey, this time to Pope John, to seek the revival of the Bishopric of Pannonia. Through the merging of the Pannonian and Moravian Bishoprics, Methodius was appointed as the Archbishop of Velehrad. However, he faced significant challenges from the Germans, who vehemently opposed the use of the Slavic language in liturgical services, despite its comprehension by the people.

As Methodius fulfilled his earthly duties, he diligently reviewed and corrected the translated books of the Bible and liturgy. On April 6, 885, this esteemed apostle of ours peacefully departed from this world, leaving a legacy of righteousness and honor. The people mourned the loss of their beloved teacher, and
Methodius was laid to rest in Velehrad.

Regrettably, the flourishing Slavic Church and its literature in Moravia, and subsequently in Bohemia, suffered severe damage at the hands of the German priests. Consequently, the disciples of Cyril and Methodius scattered, finding refuge in Bulgaria.

King Svatopluk

After the reign of Rostislav from 870 to 894, a formidable prince named Svatopluk ascended to power in Moravia. He was an exceptionally powerful ruler, commanding not only the entire Moravian territory but also vast lands encompassing present-day Slovakia, Lower Austria up to the Danube River, and many other distant regions. His realm, known as the Great Moravian Empire, stood as a testament to his strength and influence. In a time marked by turmoil and unrest, the prudent Svatopluk extended his protection to neighboring princes, defending them and their people against adversaries. Revered as a king, his laws were held in high regard, even by the Czech prince Borivoj, who recognized Svatopluk as his guardian. Whenever Svatopluk waged war, the brave Czechs wholeheartedly rallied behind him, providing unwavering support. His neighbors held him in fear, knowing that any hostile intentions would swiftly result in defeat or expulsion.

Svatopluk emerged as one of the greatest figures among the Slavic people, and had the circumstances for the Slavs been more favorable, his name would undoubtedly be revered as the nation's greatest benefactor. The profound impact of his death resonated in the hearts of the Moravian people, leaving an indelible memory that generations would continue to recount through various legends.

One of the most renowned tales is as follows:

Prince Svatopluk of Moravia commanded respect and fear from neighboring nations, known for his strength and influence. He had three sons: Mojmír, Svatopluk, and the name of the third son has been lost to history. Before his passing, Svatopluk divided his empire into three parts, assigning one portion to each of his sons. The eldest son was proclaimed the grand prince, while the other two were to be subordinate to his rule. To emphasize the importance of unity, Svatopluk presented them with three sticks bound together, instructing the eldest to break them. When he failed, the sticks were passed to the second son, and then to the third, who were able to break them individually. Seizing this moment as a teaching opportunity, Svatopluk admonished them, reminding them that as long as they remained united in love and harmony, their enemies would never overcome them or lead them into captivity. However, if they allowed differences in honor and the thirst for power to divide the kingdom into three parts, disregarding the wisdom of the first-born brother, they would persecute one another and face utter destruction at the hands of neighboring nations. Appointing his eldest son Mojmír as his successor, Svatopluk passed away in 894 with a heavy heart, foreseeing the calamities and misfortunes that would befall the land and its princes.

Unfortunately, the sons soon forgot their father's wise counsel, engaging in conflict with each other and hastening the downfall of Svatopluk's empire. The Great Moravian Empire was invaded and ravaged by the Wild Magyars, who spread across the fertile plains of Hungary. Discord and disagreement led to the loss of freedom for the people.

Christianity in Bohemia

In the ancient times, our ancestors followed pagan beliefs, worshipping a supreme God who created and protected the world. Alongside this belief, they held reverence for multiple gods and goddesses, attributing them with different powers. However, as time passed, Christianity began to gain influence among our people. Many Czechs were drawn to the moral teachings of Christians who believed in a single God, and they embraced this new faith.

During the reign of the Czech prince Bořivoj, news of the Christian religion reached his ears. When he discovered that its fundamental commandment was to love God with all one's heart, soul, strength, and mind, as well as to love one's neighbor as oneself, he was deeply impressed. A few years later, Bořivoj himself converted to Christianity, seeking to strengthen his faith. He journeyed to Moravia, where the powerful prince Svatopluk resided in Velehrad. It was there that he had the privilege of meeting the renowned Apostle of the Slavs, Methoděj. Svatopluk warmly received Bořivoj, and Saint Methoděj spoke to him about the one true God, Jesus Christ, and His teachings.

This transformative encounter opened up a new world for Bořivoj, the Czech duke, leading him to make a profound decision. He approached Saint Methoděj, requesting to be baptized, and in the year 874, this sacred event took place. Before returning to Bohemia, Bořivoj made a special request: he asked the priest Kaich to accompany him. Together, they embarked on a mission to spread the Christian faith throughout the land. Kaich traveled across Bohemia, passionately proclaiming and explaining the principles of Christianity to the people. He taught them the art of prayer, the beauty of hymns, and the act of offering sacrifices to God. He also introduced them to the sacred Christian texts, encouraging contemplation and deep reflection. The impact was profound. As the people heard the teachings, they renounced their idols, demolishing and discarding them. In their place, crosses were erected, symbolizing the new faith. The once pagan chants gave way to the resounding hymn, "Lord, have mercy," echoing in homes, churches, and fields.

The establishment of the first Christian church in Bohemia holds historical significance. It was Prince Bořivoj himself who erected this sacred place within his beloved castle, Levý Hradec, situated on a prominent rock along the left bank of the Vltava River, a three-hour journey north of Prague. The second church was constructed within Prague Castle, dedicated to the Virgin Mary's memory. These foundational churches served as beacons of the Christian faith, paving the way for its rapid spread throughout Bohemia. The seeds of piety and charity were sown, bearing abundant fruits in the hearts and lives of the people.

Saint Ivan (John)

Prince Bořivoj found solace in Tetín Castle, an architectural marvel crafted by Teta, Kroka's daughter. It was from this castle that he often embarked on exhilarating hunting expeditions in the surrounding forests. On one such occasion, his arrow struck a deer, causing it to flee and seek refuge behind a massive rock before succumbing to the pursuit of the hunting dogs. To Bořivoj's astonishment, a figure of remarkable stature emerged from the very rock—a man with flowing hair and beard, dressed in humble attire, and barefoot. In his hand, he carried a staff. Unbeknownst to the prince, this enigmatic stranger questioned why the beloved creature had met such a fate. Filled with trepidation, Bořivoj hesitated before summoning the courage to inquire if the stranger was a benevolent or malevolent spirit.

To his relief, the hermit declared himself to be a fellow human. Intrigued, Bořivoj requested to be led to the hermit's abode—a humble cave adorned with a bed of moss and leaves, draped in a coarse blanket. A cross crafted from twigs adorned the wall, and a stone served as both table and kneeling stool. It was here that the hermit, named Ivan, shared his extraordinary story. Hailing from (present day) Croatia, he had dedicated his life to the service of the Lord and Saint John the Baptist, dwelling in this secluded sanctuary for over four decades. Nourished by the abundant forest, Ivan subsisted on wild hens, forest doves, and various other birds that laid eggs for him. Forest bees provided him with honey, and the trees bore fruit. Strawberries and mushrooms were ever plentiful. Bořivoj, deeply moved by the hermit's wisdom and piety, implored him to grace Tetín Castle with his presence and offer his blessings to both Bořivoj and his devout wife, Ludmila. Ivan, in turn, vowed to honor this heartfelt request.

The following day, Prince Bořivoj, accompanied by the castle chaplain Pavel and a retinue of servants, ventured into the verdant woods to escort Ivan back to the castle. With the holy cross in hand, Ivan joined them on the journey to Tetín, where Ludmila eagerly awaited their arrival. Upon reaching the castle, Ivan bestowed his blessings upon Bořivoj's wife before retreating to his beloved cave, urging the chaplain to visit him three days hence. When the appointed day arrived, the chaplain dutifully sought out Ivan, who confided in him the story of his lineage. Born as the son of Croatian prince Gestimul and a woman named Elizabeth, Ivan willingly relinquished his birthright to his brother, feeling ill-equipped for the responsibilities of leadership. Seeking a life of undisturbed devotion to God, he sought refuge in the Bohemian forests. Sensing his impending departure from this earthly realm, Ivan requested the administration of the last sacraments, a duty fulfilled by the compassionate priest. Strengthened for his journey into eternity, Ivan entrusted the priest with the cross, entreating him to deliver it to Prince Bořivoj as a cherished memento. With his final breath, Ivan peacefully passed away.

Bořivoj, tenderly receiving the cross, kissed it reverently, overwhelmed with joy at this precious heirloom. As a testament to their encounter, Duchess Ludmila ordered the construction of a church upon the very spot where Ivan had graced their lives, ensuring his eternal memory would be enshrined in sacred space.

Today, the church built by Duchess Ludmila in honor of Saint Ivan stands as a cherished place of worship and pilgrimage. Over the centuries, it has undergone numerous renovations and modifications, but its significance remains unchanged. Known as the Church of Saint Ivan or Ivan's Church (kostel svatého Ivana), it continues to serve as a spiritual haven and a testament to the encounter between Prince Bořivoj and the saintly hermit. Situated near the rock where their fateful meeting took place, the church stands as a symbol of faith and a tangible connection to the extraordinary events that unfolded in Tetín. Visitors from near and far come to pay homage, seek solace, and contemplate the profound legacy of Saint Ivan.

Saint Ludmila

Ludmila, the wife of Bořivoj, was initially a follower of pagan beliefs. However, her life took a transformative turn when she was baptized by Saint Methodius. From that moment on, Ludmila embraced a humble and devout existence, dedicating entire nights to prayer and seeking solace in her faith. She exemplified compassion and generosity, extending help to the poor, clothing the needy, feeding the hungry, and quenching the thirst of the thirsty. Known for her kindness and selflessness, Ludmila became a mother figure to the less fortunate, offering guidance, counsel, and wisdom rooted in her deep understanding of the Lord God, Jesus Christ, and the revered Saints. Her words resonated deeply with those who sought her guidance, and her beloved grandson, Saint Wenceslaus, was especially influenced by her teachings. Ludmila, together with Wenceslaus, fervently prayed to God, guiding him to pursue goodness and justice, and to live in alignment with God's divine will.

It is often said that God bestows His presence upon those whom He loves through the symbol of the cross. In the case of Saint Ludmila, this divine love was revealed amidst trials, tribulations, and various hardships. She faced her most bitter enemy, Drahomíra, who hailed from Stodory, a land of the Lutici in Brandenburg, and remained a pagan. After the untimely death of her virtuous husband, Vratislav, Ludmila's son, Drahomíra ascended to the position of Czech princess and began persecuting Ludmila, spurred on by some nobles at court. In the face of such adversity, the devout and greatly afflicted duchess sought solace and refuge at her Tetín Castle, where she dedicated herself to fervent prayer and communion with God.

Indeed, prayer acts as a shield for the soul, providing strength and resilience in times of temptation, as well as comfort and tranquility during persecution. However, even within the sanctuary of Tetín, Drahomíra continued to harbor a deep hatred towards Ludmila, going so far as to commit the most heinous act imaginable— murdering the gentle and virtuous Ludmila. This act of godlessness is truly deplorable. Sending two ruthless assassins from Prague to Tetín under the cover of night, Drahomíra aimed to carry out her wicked plan. Despite their efforts, they found the castle gates securely closed. Determined, they forcibly broke open the gates and stormed into Ludmila's chamber. There, they discovered Ludmila on her knees, fervently praying beneath the symbol of the cross, her hands raised in devotion to the Redeemer.

Tragically, even in this sacred moment, the cruel assassins showed no mercy to the gentle soul. They used her own veil to suffocate her (September 15, 921). At the break of dawn, when the crime was discovered, a profound sense of grief and sorrow swept across the land as the people mourned the loss of their kind-hearted mother.

Soon after committing this heinous act, Drahomíra was consumed by remorse and sought redemption. To atone for her sins, she ordered the conversion of the very house where the murder occurred into the Church of Saint Michael the Archangel. Recognizing the sanctity of the place, it served as a poignant reminder of the tragic event that had transpired. Meanwhile, the body of the holy martyr, Ludmila, was eventually transferred from Tetín to Prague, where she found her final resting place in the Church of Saint George. Justice, too, caught up with the perpetrators of this terrible crime. One of them met his demise alongside his companions, while the other, unable to escape his guilt, fled abroad never to return. It is a testament to the justice of God that evil deeds are ultimately met with retribution, even if time has passed.

In those times, people strongly believed that the eternal battle between darkness and light extended beyond earthly conflicts and encompassed the realm of spirituality. They understood that the forces of evil would often oppose those who sought to uphold goodness and righteousness. This belief served as a reminder of the enduring importance of faith and the need for individuals to stand firm in their convictions, knowing that their actions and sacrifices held profound significance in the eternal struggle between darkness and light.

The saints, in their pursuit of virtue, often faced suffering, opposition and schemes designed to undermine their righteousness. Yet, as Jesus proclaimed, "Whoever loses their life for my sake will find it," signifying the promise of eternal life that awaits those who remain steadfast in their faith, even in the face of adversity.

Saint Wenceslas

Saint Wenceslas, the grandson of Saint Ludmila, inherited all the virtues of her kind heart, as she had raised him. He could not have received a better inheritance.

According to legend, as a young boy, he actively participated in the Holy Sacrifice, serving alongside the priest. It was during these sacred moments that he would distribute loaves of bread to the poor, lovingly prepared by his grandmother. Embracing the compassionate spirit instilled in him, Wenceslas, as the Duke of Bohemia, dedicated himself to alleviating the suffering of the less fortunate. He provided food and clothing to the destitute, extended care to orphans and widows, and even paid for the freedom of prisoners and captives. Moreover, he played a pivotal role in building churches and schools, establishing vineyards and gardens that brought prosperity and knowledge to his realm.

During Wenceslas's reign, King Henry the Fowler held sway over Germany and constantly sought to expand his dominion by waging war against the

Polabian Slavs. His ambitions went beyond merely subjugating the Czechs' neighbors; he aimed to humble our ancestors and subject them to his rule. In 928, alongside Duke Arnulf of Bavaria, he launched an invasion of Bohemia, pushing his forces as far as Prague in 929. Faced with overwhelming odds, Wenceslas made a difficult decision to secure peace and protect his people. He pledged to pay an annual tribute of 500 silver hřivnas and 120 oxen to the German king.

Many nobles expressed discontent with this arrangement and criticized Wenceslas for appearing submissive to the Germans. Some of these dissatisfied nobles joined forces with Boleslav, Wenceslas's younger brother, who governed the region known today as Stará Boleslav. Boleslav possessed a vastly different temperament compared to Wenceslas – he was proud, daring, and driven by a strong ambition for power.

In an effort to better understand the needs of his subjects, Wenceslas embarked on visits to various towns in his realm during the annual celebrations of their church consecrations. On September 27, 935, he journeyed to Stará Boleslav accompanied by his loyal servant, Podiven, intending to pay a visit to his brother. Along the way, he encountered a rider who, upon recognizing him, dismounted and approached the prince with great respect. The rider urgently pleaded with Wenceslas, saying,

"Oh, our lord and prince! You must return home swiftly, for your brother seeks your life. Please mount my horse and make your way back to Prague." Reluctant to believe that his own brother could harbor such cruelty, Wenceslas hesitated, pondering in his heart that not even a single hair on his head could be harmed without the knowledge of his Heavenly Father. As Wenceslas drew closer, Boleslav appeared at the castle, wearing a friendly expression upon his face.

After the church ceremonies concluded, Wenceslas planned to return to Prague, but upon Boleslav's request, he agreed to stay for the prepared feast. When the next day arrived, Wenceslas followed his customary routine, rising early and hurrying to the morning prayer in the church. As he approached the gates, he greeted his brother with kindness, expressing gratitude, and saying, "Our host was gracious to us last night."

However, to Wenceslas's shock, Boleslav drew his sword and, with a furious voice, declared, "I will treat you even better today." He struck Wenceslas on the head with the sword, but the blow did not prove fatal. In a display of strength, Wenceslas seized his brother, wrestled the sword from his grip, and knocked him to the ground. With deep compassion, Wenceslas uttered, "May God forgive you, my brother! I could spill your blood now, but I choose not to, for God would hold me accountable on the Day of Judgment."

Despite his merciful words, Boleslav began to scream as if Wenceslas intended to end his life. This prompted Boleslav's servants – Česta, Tyra, and Hněvsa – to rush aggressively towards Wenceslas. Wounded and in retreat, Wenceslas sought sanctuary in the church, where he fell at the entrance, pierced by Hněvsa's sword on September 28. With his final breath, Wenceslas surrendered his spirit, uttering, "Into Your hands, O Lord, I entrust my soul."

Boleslav's heinous act plunged the entire Czech land into mourning. Even Drahomíra herself rushed to the scene, weeping inconsolably as she threw herself upon her son's lifeless body. Unable to remain in the house where the murder occurred and where her own life was threatened, she fled to Charvát's land near the upper Jizera River.

The solemn burial of Saint Wenceslas took place at a later time. Three years after the tragic event, Boleslav ordered the exhumation of his slain brother's body in Boleslav. With profound reverence and the unanimous support of the people, the remains were transferred to Prague Castle, specifically to the crypt of Saint Vitus Cathedral. It was in that very spot that Saint Wenceslas himself had declared, "I will build this church!" His final resting place was chosen to be on the right side of the altar, among the twelve apostles, as a lasting testament to his legacy.

Just as the Czech people revered and cherished him during his lifetime as a true father to his subjects, they continue to invoke his name after his death as the martyr of the Lord and the patron saint of the Czech land. During the coronation of Czech kings, many deserving individuals are honored as "Knights of Saint Wenceslas." The Czech people turn to Saint Wenceslas in times of need, especially in battles, a testament to his courageous spirit. His image adorns banners, coins, and pennants, symbolizing his enduring presence. The precious relics of Saint Wenceslas, along with his helmet, sword, and chainmail, are preserved in Prague's Chapel of Saint Wenceslas within Saint Vitus Cathedral.

For centuries, a beautiful song has been sung, carrying the timeless words:

Saint Wenceslas, ruler of the Czech land,
Our prince! Intercede for us before God,
Saint Wenceslas, Kyrie eleison!

You are the heir of the Czech land,
Remember your people.
Do not let us perish, nor future generations,
Saint Wenceslas, Christ, have mercy!

We ask for your help,
Have mercy on us!
Comfort the sorrowful, drive away all evil,
Saint Wenceslas, Kyrie eleison!

The heavenly kingdom is beautiful,
Blessed are those who reach it,
Eternal life, radiant fire,
Holy Spirit, Christ, have mercy, and so on.

Original Czech:

Svatý Václave, vévodo české země,
Kníže náš, nedej zahynouti nám,
I bud' v budoucnosti vždy vítěznémě,
Do tvého království doved nás,
Svatý Václave, Kriste, eleison!

Jsi dědicem české země vlastní,
Lid svůj nezapomeň a pros za něj,
Nechte nezahynouti v budoucnosti,
Svatý Václave, Kriste, smiluj se nám!

O pomoc prosíme Tebe s nadějí,
Smiluj se nad námi, Václave náš,
Utěš nám truchlivým srdce ztrhané,
Zahlad' vše zlé, Svatý Václave, eleison!

Království nebeské krásné jest věru,
Blahoslavení, kdo tam dojdou všichni,
Věčný život, jasný oheň a Svatý Duch,
Kriste, smiluj se, Svatý Václave, eleison!

Founding of St. Vitus Cathedral

During the time of Saint Wenceslas, two churches already stood within the walls of Prague Castle, each with its own significance. One was erected by Bořivoj in honor of the Virgin Mary, while the other was established by Prince Vratislav to honor Saint George, who found his final resting place there. The latter church also housed the remains of the first Czech martyr, Saint Ludmila, whose devout grandson, Václav, had her transferred from Tetín to this sacred site.

However, Saint Wenceslas's devotion and desire to create a magnificent place of worship led him to build a third church alongside these existing ones. Dedicated to Saint Vitus, this extraordinary project was marked by the saint's unwavering commitment and immense resources. He personally supervised the daily progress of construction, eagerly anticipating the moment when he could enter the completed church and offer his prayers. In time, this remarkable edifice not only became the largest but also the most affluent church in all of Bohemia.

The establishment of this church received official approval from the Bishop of Prague through a special decree. Once completed, it was consecrated with grandeur and magnificence, radiating with the gleam of precious metals. Its unique round shape added to its splendor, while the main altar was dedicated to Saint Vitus, bestowing upon it even greater significance.

The honor bestowed upon this church continued to grow. Boleslav I, recognizing the sanctity of his brother, arranged for the transfer of Saint Wenceslas's remains to this revered place. Now, he could pray for forgiveness at his tomb within the confines of this beloved sanctuary. Saint Wenceslas found his eternal rest in the chapel to the right of the altar of the twelve holy apostles, accompanied by his loyal servant, Podivín.

Through the years, the Czech people have held St. Vitus Cathedral in deep reverence. It underwent further renovations and reconstructions under the care of Charles I, with utmost respect for the remains of other revered saints, including St. Adalbert and St. John of Nepomuk, who also find their eternal repose within its sacred walls.

Boleslav I and II

After the passing of Saint Wenceslas, Boleslav the Cruel[4] ascended to the role of Duke of Bohemia. He made a bold decision, refusing to comply with King Henry's demand to send cattle and money to the Germans, a commitment that Wenceslas had previously agreed to. This act of defiance sparked the wrath of the Germans, leading to a prolonged war that spanned over fourteen years. The new German king, Otto I, dispatched two formidable armies, the Thuringians and the Saxons, to confront Boleslav and his forces in Bohemia.

---

[4] Duke Boleslav I greatly increased the obedience of the common people and introduced forced labor and uniform laws in the execution of justice. However, his reforms were not implemented in a gentle and voluntary manner but often through force. This went against the cherished ancient freedom of the Slavs and their unrestrained nature. Moreover, many, due to their short-sightedness, failed to see the purpose behind it all. It is easy to imagine why Boleslav I was remembered by his contemporaries as "the Cruel."

Undeterred by the formidable opposition, Boleslav fearlessly engaged the Thuringians in battle, emerging victorious and expelling them from Czech lands. He then swiftly shifted his attention to the Saxons, employing a strategic ambush that resulted in their resounding defeat. Asik, their leader, met his demise at the hands of Boleslav.

However, the tide turned against the Czechs in the year 950 when King Otto himself, accompanied by a massive army, launched a formidable invasion deep into the heart of Bohemia. The city of Prague faced a prolonged siege, and Boleslav, recognizing the dire circumstances, ultimately had to yield. In order to secure peace, he agreed to resume payment of tribute to King Otto and pledged his assistance against the Hungarian forces.

The Hungarians, a nomadic nation from Asia, had settled in Hungary after the death of Svatopluk. From there, they launched raids into neighboring lands, including Germany. King Otto of Germany could no longer tolerate their actions and declared war against them. In a show of solidarity, Boleslav sent a well-armed contingent of a thousand Czech warriors to support Otto's cause. The decisive battle took place at the Augsburg Plain, near the Lech River in present-day Bavaria, in 955.

The clash was fierce, and the outcome was resounding. The Hungarians suffered a complete defeat and were forced to retreat. The loss of life was devastating. During their retreat, the Hungarian leaders gathered to discuss their next move, realizing that returning home empty-handed would bring great shame upon them. They devised a plan to attack the Czech lands and plunder whatever they could find. However, they underestimated the courage and strategic prowess of Boleslav.

Boleslav and his army awaited the Hungarian invaders at the borders, concealed in forested ambushes. They valiantly defended their lands and inflicted even greater losses on the Hungarians than before. Boleslav managed to capture Lehé, the Hungarian leader. From that point onward, the Hungarians dared not invade Czech lands and ceased their plundering raids to the west. Boleslav I earned immense merit not only for the Czech lands but also for fostering peace and stability within Western Christianity.

Boleslav continued his military campaigns, expanding his domain to include Moravia, Slovakia, Silesia, and Belocharvatsko. This laid the foundation for a new and powerful West Slavic empire, which his son Boleslav II further expanded. The Czech empire now found itself neighboring the Great Prince of Kiev in Russia. The conversion of the Poles to Christianity was accomplished through the efforts of Princess Dubravka, Boleslav's daughter, who married Mieszko, the Polish prince. The other children of

Boleslav were also deeply devout. Strachkvas, also known as Kristan, became a monk and chronicled the history of his time. Princess Mlada, or Milada as she was called in Latin, entered a monastery and became the abbess, leading the first virgin monastery in Bohemia.

Boleslav, the successor to the throne, earned the title of Pious due to his repentant spirit. The people forgave him for his past transgressions, recognizing his sincere remorse and diligent efforts to promote the well-being of his subjects. At his death in 967, Bohemia stood stronger and more powerful than ever before.

Saint Adalbert

Boleslav the Pious was a deeply compassionate and devout ruler. He dedicated himself to the construction of numerous churches, the establishment of monasteries and schools, and the generous support of the poor through acts of charity. Despite the vastness of his kingdom, the need for a specific ecclesiastical administration arose. To address this, Boleslav founded the Prague bishopric in 973.

The first appointed Bishop of Prague was a Benedictine monk named Dětmar. Originally from Saxony, he had resided in Bohemia for an extended period and was well-versed in the Czech language. Dětmar was a highly educated and pious man. Upon his passing, the Czech people elected Vojtěch as their bishop.

Vojtěch[5], born into the Slavník family, who held prominence in the Libice Castle overlooking the Cidlina and Elbe rivers, came from a wealthy

---

[5] Adalbert of Prague (Czech: svatý Vojtěch).

background. His devout mother and his first foster father, the priest Radla, ensured that he was raised in a godly manner. Later, he was sent to the prestigious school in Magdeburg, where his dedication and diligence surpassed that of his peers. Upon reaching adulthood, Vojtěch was ordained as a priest by Bishop Adalbert of Magdeburg, who bestowed upon him his own name. However, the Czech people continued to address him as Vojtěch.

As a bishop, Vojtěch devoted himself to strengthening Christianity in Bohemia. He sought to instill good manners and customs among the people, leading by example with his own virtuous life. He selflessly used a mere quarter of the bishop's income for his personal needs, while the remainder was dedicated to building churches and providing assistance to the poor. He acted as a caring father to widows and orphans, earning a reputation for his compassion and righteousness. People regarded him as a saintly figure even during his lifetime.

During his extensive travels throughout his diocese, which stretched as far as Slovakia and the Danube region, Vojtěch found himself near Esztergom, the residence of Hungarian prince Géza. Impressed by his virtues, Géza sent a splendid invitation for Vojtěch to visit his court. The bishop accepted and had the privilege of baptizing Géza's young son, Vajk, who later adopted the name Štěpán (Stephen) and became the apostle of his people.

However, back in Bohemia, some people were reluctant to abandon certain pagan customs. In response, Vojtěch decided to travel to Rome. There, he entered a monastery and bestowed blessings upon those who had harmed him. Yet, the Czechs soon recognized their error and fervently pleaded for his return. They promised to heed his teachings. Granting their request, Saint Vojtěch came back to his homeland after a three-year absence.

At his request, the first male Benedictine monastery in Břevnov near Prague was established in Bohemia. Additionally, the Czech assembly enacted new laws to establish a tithe for the bishopric, ensuring the necessary support for the maintenance of churches and other matters. However, when conflicts and resistance arose again from those unwilling to fully abandon their pagan customs, the compassionate Vojtěch made the decision to return to Rome once more.

At the request of the Holy Father, Vojtěch intended to make his second return to Prague. However, upon reaching the borders of the Czech land, he received distressing news. The powerful and wealthy Vršovci family had killed his brothers, who had sought assistance against Prince Boleslav and the Vršovci while they were abroad in the court of Emperor Otto III and Polish Boleslav. Devastated by this tragedy, Vojtěch made the difficult decision not to proceed to Bohemia. Instead, he embarked on a mission to preach the word of God to the pagan Prussians, who were part of the Lithuanian tribe.

Accompanied by the priest Benedikt and his own devoted brother Radim, who had wholeheartedly dedicated himself to Vojtěch, they ventured to convert the Prussians to the Christian faith. Vojtěch succeeded in bringing many of them to embrace Christianity. However, a significant portion of the Prussian nation rejected Vojtěch's teachings and even posed threats of violence and death towards him. Despite the challenges and opposition he faced, Vojtěch remained steadfast in his mission to spread the message of God's love and grace.

After enduring relentless persecution, Vojtěch found himself in Samland, also known as the Land of Samogitia, located near the Baltic Sea in present-day Kaliningrad. It was midday when he and his companions arrived at a vast field known as Romové, considered sacred by the pagan people. Despite their weariness, they gathered to celebrate Holy Mass, with Vojtěch receiving Holy Communion. After the prayers, they sought some rest to rejuvenate their exhausted bodies.

However, their peaceful reprieve was abruptly interrupted by wild cries. A furious mob of pagans descended upon them, swiftly binding them with ropes and taking them captive. Vojtěch, remaining steadfast, encouraged his companions to endure the trials, while he himself turned to prayer, expressing gratitude to God for the opportunity to suffer for His sake. In that critical moment, a pagan priest forcefully thrust a deadly spear into Vojtěch's chest, with others joining in the cruel act. Bleeding from seven wounds, Vojtěch lifted his eyes towards heaven, offering prayers for his enemies, as his spirit departed from his mortal body on April 23, 997. The pagans proceeded to sever his head and dismember his remains.

Vojtěch's brother Radim and the priest were spared and managed to escape, seeking refuge with Polish Prince Boleslav. They informed him about the martyrdom of the bishop. Boleslav, recognizing the significance of Vojtěch's sacrifice, spared no expense in redeeming his body and arranging a grand burial in Gniezno, his main residence. Later, Vojtěch's remains were brought to Prague and laid to rest with great reverence in the St. Vitus Cathedral.

Sons of Boleslav II

Boleslav II, who was affectionately known as "the Pious and Generous" among the Czechs, had three sons: Boleslav, Jaromír, and Oldřich. The vast West Slavic realm established by Boleslav II had the potential to flourish and achieve even greater power and glory if his sons had maintained brotherly love and unity. Moreover, if the eldest among them, who was called to assume supreme leadership, had followed the noble example set by their father and wise grandfather.

Regrettably, our nation faced a great misfortune with the emergence of Boleslav III, also known as "the Redhead," who proved to be a despicable scoundrel. Influenced by the ill advice of the Vršovice clan, he caused immense harm to the Czech people, his own family, and ultimately brought about his own downfall due to his insatiable greed and incompetence. Unfortunately, it is not always the case that worthy parents are blessed with worthy children who carry on their legacy, preserving and elevating the family's wealth and honorable name inherited from their ancestors.

The magnitude of this misfortune was magnified by the fact that wise rulers governed the neighboring realms during that time. Boleslav the Brave held the reins in Poland, the son of Měčislav and Czech Dúbravka. Vladimir the Great led Russia, while Saint Stephen emerged as a luminary in Hungary. Germany, too, witnessed the rule of Otto III and, following his untimely demise, the reign of Saint Henry. The Czechs, unfortunately, did not enjoy the same fortune during Boleslav III's tumultuous reign.

Boleslav the Brave, the King of Poland and a relative of Boleslav the Redhead through his mother Dúbravka, wasted no time in recognizing the incompetence of his cousin. Immediately following the passing of Boleslav II, he led his army into the easternmost part of the Czech realm, specifically Kraków. The Czech garrison stationed in Kraków fought bravely, but their valiant efforts were not enough to withstand the enemy's onslaught. The Czech army was severely outnumbered, and to worsen matters, Boleslav the Redhead, who remained idle in Prague, failed to send reinforcements. He neglected to acknowledge the impending danger that loomed over his eastern territories, as he was too preoccupied with his internal conflicts against his two brothers[6]. Envious of the lands in Bohemia that their father had allocated to them as their princely domains under his rule, Boleslav the Redhead pursued a vengeful agenda. His two brothers, along with their mother Emma, were forced to flee from Bohemia to Bavaria in order to escape his wrath.

Meanwhile, Boleslav the Brave swiftly expanded his dominion by conquering Moravia, Silesia, and Slovakia with his military might. As a result, within a year, the Czech kingdom was reduced to its smallest extent, limited to the land of Bohemia alone. The truth of the saying "He who desires what is foreign loses what is his own" became evident in the case of the avaricious Boleslav III.

It is not difficult to imagine that a person who shows no compassion to his own family members would not exhibit noble behavior towards others. Boleslav the Redhead displayed cruelty towards his subjects and anyone who failed to meet his

---

[6] Jaromír took control of the expansive Hradec district, where he established a stronghold that eventually developed into the town of Jaroměř nad Labem. Meanwhile, Oldřich governed the territory formerly belonging to the Zličan princes. He constructed the Oldříš Castle along the banks of the Elbe River, situated between Libice and present-day Kolín. Today, the village of Podhradí occupies that location, serving as a reminder of the castle's historical presence.

exacting demands. Even his advisors and former allies, the Vršovice clan, experienced his ruthless nature. The fleeting nature of wicked alliances became evident. They convinced the Czech people to expel Boleslav from the country and instead enthrone Vladivoj, the younger brother of Boleslav the Brave and the son of Czech Dubravka. This momentous change occurred, and Boleslav III, known as Ryšavec, managed to save his own life by swiftly fleeing from Bohemia.

The Czech homeland now faced a perilous period, as the threat of losing its independence and falling under the dominion of powerful neighboring empires, be it German or Polish, loomed large.

Vladivoj understood that following the expulsion of Boleslav the Redhead from Bohemia, the rightful claim to the throne lay with one of his younger brothers, either Jaromír or Oldřich. However, the Vršovice clan advised against appointing them as rulers, fearing potential retaliation for the injustices they had suffered in the past. Seeking a powerful protector, Vladivoj journeyed to Germany alongside his own brother, Boleslav the Brave, who was also facing difficulties. Their aim was to place themselves and the land of Bohemia under the authority of German King Henry. This decision set a negative precedent, as many members of the Přemyslid dynasty would later attempt to seize power from stronger relatives in Bohemia.

Regrettably, Vladivoj's reign was short-lived, lasting only a few months before his untimely death. Subsequently, the Czech people turned to Jaromír to assume the throne. However, he too was forced to flee the country soon after. Boleslav the Brave, using military might, brought Ryšavec (Boleslav III) back to Bohemia, offering him protection as Ryšavec sought refuge. The shrewd Boleslav the Brave anticipated that Ryšavec's cruelty would soon alienate the Czechs, positioning himself as their liberator once Ryšavec's favor dwindled.

And so it happened: In the waning days of Carnival in 1003, Boleslav the Brave issued the order to massacre all those who had previously expelled him from the land. Upon receiving this news, the Czechs reached out to Boleslav the Brave, who wasted no time in apprehending Ryšavec (Boleslav III) and blinding him. He swiftly made his way to Prague, ready to seize power for himself.

However, the German King Henry II harbored concerns over the growing strength of Boleslav the Brave's kingdom. He feared having a neighbor who wielded too much influence. To address this, King Henry sent a message proposing that he would recognize Boleslav the Brave as the Prince of Bohemia on the condition that Bohemia became a fief under his rule. Yet, Boleslav the Brave declined this offer, prompting King Henry to pledge his support to Jaromír instead. Both Přemyslids, Jaromír and Oldřich, then launched an invasion of Prague, driving out the Polish forces that had pillaged the city and fallen out of favor with the Czechs. Jaromír assumed the role of prince, while Oldřich received the principality of Lutsk along the Ohře River as his share.

It would have been ideal for our homeland if the two brothers could have lived in harmony. However, driven by ambition, Oldřich was not content with his share. After a few years, he stripped Jaromír of power, took the princely throne for himself, and imprisoned his own brother.

Prince Oldřich had a profound passion for hunting, and on two occasions, something significant occurred during his pursuits in the wilderness.

The first instance took place when he still ruled only over Lutsk. While riding from his castle Drahouše above the Ohře River, which is now where the town of Postoloprty stands, Oldřich embarked on a hunt in the dense forests nearby, stretching between the Ohře and Berounka rivers. On his return from the hunt, he stumbled upon a picturesque scene—a young woman named Božena, the daughter of nobleman Křesina, washing clothes by a well in a small village. Enchanted by her beauty and noble demeanor, Oldřich decided to marry her.

Many years later, when Oldřich had ascended to the position of Prince of Bohemia, he found himself on another hunting expedition in the forests above the Sázava River. It was there that he came across a priest named Prokop, leading a hermit's life similar to St. John above the Berounka. Oldřich developed a deep admiration for Prokop and appointed him as his confessor. As an act of penance for his transgressions, especially those committed against his brother Jaromír, Oldřich commissioned the construction of a Benedictine monastery above the Sázava River. The monastery would conduct divine services in the Slavic language, with Prokop serving as its first abbot.

Břetislav I

Oldřich and Božena were blessed with a son named Břetislav, a courageous young man who gained immense renown for his bravery even during his father's lifetime and reign.

Following the passing of Boleslav the Brave in 1025, similar disputes erupted within the ruling family of Poland. One of the factions sought the intervention of Stephen, the King of Hungary, in the Polish affairs. As a result, Moravia and Slovakia were detached from the Polish realm. However, the fearless Czech prince Břetislav, son of Oldřich, recognized that these lands had been wrongfully seized by Boleslav the Brave. Determined to reclaim what rightfully belonged to the Czechs, he led his brave warriors into battle against both the Poles and the Hungarians, successfully regaining control over Moravia. However, Slovakia remained aligned with Hungary, and that alliance persists to this day.

Having achieved victory, Břetislav embarked on a meaningful journey to the ancient sacred site of

Velehrad. Overwhelmed by grief at its destruction, he shed tears for its loss. In a gesture of devotion, he dedicated the abundant spoils of war, including the treasures he had seized from the Hungarians, to the restoration of the holy sanctuary of Velehrad.

After the passing of his father in 1037, Břetislav ascended to the position of Prince of Bohemia. However, the Czech lands felt too confined for his ambitions, and he yearned to establish a grand empire. Gathering an army, he embarked on an invasion of Polish territory, seizing valuable treasures such as exquisite paintings and majestic bells. Loading them onto wagons, he triumphantly brought them back to Prague. Yet, the Czech people did not display as much elation over these spoils as they did over the sacred remains of St. Vojtěch (Adalbert).

Selected soldiers, having observed a three-day fast and engaged in profound penance, were entrusted with the solemn task of elevating the revered body. A massive crowd from Prague poured out to meet them, with Bishop Sebiř (Severius) and Prince Břetislav personally carrying the martyr's remains to the St. Vitus Cathedral. The priests bore a magnificent golden cross, crafted by Boleslav the Brave, the King of Poland, adorned with three layers of gold. Among the procession were also numerous jewels crafted from gold and precious stones, serving as plunder from Poland.

However, Pope Benedict IX and Henry III, the King of Germany, admonished Břetislav to return all the treasures he had seized from Polish territory. Břetislav, however, adamantly refused, leading to a declaration of war. In the year 1040, two formidable German armies launched an invasion of Bohemia. The first, under the leadership of the German king himself, advanced through the Šumava Mountains. Prince Břetislav fearlessly confronted them and achieved a resounding victory near Domažlice in the Šumava Forest. To commemorate this triumph, the Czech people erected a chapel dedicated to St. Wenceslas. Meanwhile, the second army, overwhelmed by fear of Břetislav, swiftly retreated from Bohemia.

However, the following year, King Henry arrived with two even more formidable armies. The first army skillfully circumvented the Czech encampment, aided by a German hermit residing in the Šumava Mountains who revealed secret paths, allowing them to march directly towards Prague. Determined to resist with unwavering resolve, Břetislav commanded the governor of Bílina, Prkos, to hold back the second German army at the northern borders. Regrettably, Prkos succumbed to German bribery, betraying his own people by allowing the enemy to enter Bohemian territory unchallenged.

Deeply betrayed and filled with a sense of shame, Břetislav was left with no choice but to pursue peace. He relinquished his claim to Poland and consented to pay an annual tribute. However, the treacherous Prkos did not escape the retribution he deserved. Incensed warriors apprehended him, severing his hands and feet before casting him into the depths of the Bílina River.

As a gesture of compensation for acquiring the body of St. Vojtěch (Adalbert) and numerous precious church treasures from Poland, Břetislav erected the Church of St. Wenceslas in Stará Boleslav.

During his rule, Břetislav governed with wisdom and prudence. He enacted a multitude of enlightened laws and established a tradition dictating that the eldest member of the Přemyslid dynasty would always assume the role of prince, while other male descendants would receive estates in Moravia under his supreme authority.

Spytihněv II

Spytihněv II, the prince, possessed a strikingly handsome appearance and ruled his subjects with wisdom, employing a balance of firmness and kindness. In every sense, he epitomized a man of utmost worth and nobility. Regrettably, he succumbed to ill advice that led to the expulsion of Slavic monks from the monastery near the Sázava River, replacing them with the Latin rite.

One incident showcasing his commitment to justice unfolded on a day when he was preparing to lead his troops into battle, unaware of the impending enemy they would confront. Amidst the preparations, a distraught widow approached him, tears streaming down her face, and clasped onto his horse's stirrups.

With desperation in her voice, she pleaded, "My lord, have mercy upon me, a poor widow. Administer justice and protect me from my adversaries." Spytihněv responded, "I shall gladly do so upon my return from battle, for it is not fitting for me to abandon my people." The widow beseeched further, "But if you do not return, who shall I turn to for safeguard? The people may not require your presence in battle today, yet I, a sorrowful woman, implore you for justice. By granting it, you shall receive God's grace and be richly rewarded."

The prince contemplated her words and replied, "Dear woman, if I cannot render justice before my return, my officials shall attend to it on your behalf."

She bowed respectfully and voiced, "Gracious lord, why defer to others? Why deny yourself the reward that you seek from God in every deed and instead bestow it upon someone else?"

With resolve, Spytihněv dismounted from his horse, summoned the judges, and called forth the accused party mentioned by the widow. Right then and there, a makeshift court session commenced. He attentively listened to the case, recognized the justness of the widow's claim, and commanded the guilty party to be punished and restore what rightfully belonged to her.

During the reign of Spytihněv II, the fervent devotion of Christians swelled to such an extent that the grandeur of St. Vitus Cathedral in Prague could no longer accommodate them all. Recognizing this, Prince Spytihněv took the initiative to expand and enhance the Church of St. Vitus, including the chapel dedicated to St.

Vojtěch (Adalbert). With unwavering zeal, he oversaw the construction, ensuring its swift completion. Sadly, before the project reached its culmination, fate dealt a cruel blow, as Spytihněv fell ill and passed away, prematurely departing from his role as the ruler of Bohemia after a brief but impactful reign of merely six years. The Czech people, profoundly grief-stricken by the loss of this noble duke, bestowed upon him the title of the father of priests and the guardian of widows and orphans, acknowledging his unwavering dedication to their welfare.

Vratislav II

Vratislav II, the elder brother of Spytihněv and former prince of Olomouc, ascended to the position of prince of Bohemia. He was known for his courage, valor, and remarkable generosity.

This period in history was marked by immense upheaval across Europe. Wars raged incessantly, as each ruler sought dominion over others, while few were willing to heed the counsel of others. Amidst these tumultuous times, our own Vratislav stood steadfastly by the side of Henry IV, the German king. The Czech warriors fearlessly aided the king in numerous pivotal battles, with their notable contribution including being among the first to breach the formidable walls of the city of Leonova following a prolonged siege in 1083.

In return, the king granted Vratislav a pardon from the annual tribute, instead requesting 300 armed men to provide assistance whenever he marched to Rome. When Vratislav attended the assembly in Mainz in 1086, the grateful king bestowed upon him the crown, elevating him to the position of the Czech king.

This news brought immense joy to the Czech people, who held a deep affection for their beloved king Vratislav. Those who were able hurried to the city of Prague, their homeland, to witness the unprecedented celebration in Bohemia. On the sacred feast day of St. Vitus, Vratislav and his wife Svatava, adorned in regal attire, were anointed and crowned in the presence of numerous princes, bishops, nobles, and a multitude of people at St. Vitus Cathedral. As the Archbishop of Trier placed the crown upon Vratislav's head, the entire Czech population erupted in exultation, proclaiming, "Blessings, victory, and glory to Vratislav, the anointed king of Bohemia and Poland, chosen by God, benevolent and gracious!" The festivities that ensued were nothing short of grand, filled with merriment and unbounded jubilation.

Břetislav II

King Henry IV expressed his gratitude for the unwavering loyalty of our fearless Vratislav by bestowing upon him the region of Meissen as a reward. In 1087, King Vratislav embarked on a journey to this new territory to negotiate its borders with his Saxon neighbors. However, the Saxons were reluctant to cede any land, resulting in the outbreak of a war. In this conflict, Vratislav entrusted his son Břetislav, a remarkably brave young man, with the task of leading the charge against the enemy.

Břetislav's march with his army was far from futile, especially when it came to confronting a particular town whose inhabitants had previously caused trouble for Vratislav during his return from the imperial court. Břetislav took decisive action by setting the town ablaze and seizing any valuable resources found within. Having accomplished this mission, he eagerly returned to his father, eagerly anticipating the astonishment of the Czech people upon witnessing the vast spoils of war and the substantial number of captured livestock that accompanied him. With the wagons leading the way and the Czech warriors following closely behind, they reached a tranquil stream around noon.

Prince Břetislav gave the command for the vanguard to press forward while he and a smaller group of lords decided to pause by the stream for lunch and rest. It was a scorching day in July, prompting Břetislav to strip off his armor and garments, immersing himself in the cool waters to refresh his body. As he lingered there, Aleksa, a respected leader of the Czech people, approached him with an important message. Aleksa warned the prince against bathing in foreign and hostile waters, urging him to instead bathe in the familiar waters of their own Czech land, such as the Vltava or the Ohře. He emphasized the need for haste, as Břetislav possessed Saxon spoils that could be reclaimed by the enemy. In response, Břetislav confidently replied, "I am well aware that older individuals are often frightened by even the slightest noise, and much more so by the prospect of death for the young." Aleksa retorted, "May God grant us an opportunity for battle, without harm befalling our people, and then we shall see whether it is the old or the young who fear death more."

In that very moment, approximately twenty Saxon horsemen emerged, positioning themselves to launch an attack on the small contingent of Czech warriors who had fallen behind the others. Witnessing this imminent threat, the Czech lords who accompanied Břetislav swiftly mounted their horses and engaged the Saxons in combat, disregarding Aleksa's attempts to halt them. However, as the battle commenced, a significantly larger group of Saxon soldiers emerged from an ambush and savagely slaughtered those valiant Czech warriors. With a billowing cloud of dust signaling the approach of even more Saxons, the main Czech army was alerted to the dire situation. Aleksa, as the leader of the army, promptly commanded his forces to stand firm and fight back, initiating a fierce clash. Spears splintered upon impact, swords clashed in a brutal exchange, and the cacophony of weapons and resounding battle cries filled the air. In the face of overwhelming odds, the Saxons eventually turned and fled, compelled to retreat by the relentless determination of the Czechs, despite their numerical disadvantage. The victory came at a high cost, with the ground stained by the blood of the brave.

The main body of the army had already departed with the spoils, leaving behind only the lords and warriors who had chosen to remain with the prince and engage in the battle. Tragically, this decision resulted in the loss of many lives and countless injuries. Among the fallen were esteemed leaders such as Aleksa, Ratibor (his son-in-law), Brániš, and Slava. Additionally, the brave župan Přidá, though gravely wounded with a severed leg, managed to narrowly escape death. Břetislav himself suffered a severe wound under his left arm, narrowly saved from losing his entire arm by his firm grip on his sword. It was the impetuousness of this young prince that led to the deaths of many respected individuals and inflicted injuries upon countless others. Oh, if only he had sought the counsel of the wise elders!

In the year 1100, tragedy struck again. Břetislav was partaking in a hunting expedition within the dense Křivoklát forests when he fell victim to a treacherous act of hired assassination during the dark of night. The assassin ruthlessly stabbed Břetislav in the abdomen, inflicting a fatal wound. Two days later, at Zbečno, the courageous prince succumbed to his injuries, and his body was subsequently transported to Prague for burial.

Extinction of the Vršovice Family

In recorded history, we often find that divine justice prevails, punishing transgressors in a manner mirroring their own deeds. Such was the case with the Vršovice family, an esteemed and influential lineage in Bohemia, who perpetrated a treacherous and cruel extermination of the Slavníkovice family—a prominent and prosperous lineage, from which the revered St. Vojtěch originated.

In the year 1108, Czech prince Svatopluk, extending aid to Henry V, the German king, in his conflict against Coloman, the Hungarian king, entrusted the safeguarding of Bohemia to Count Vacek and the Vršovice family. Regrettably, soon after Svatopluk's departure from Bohemia, Boleslav of Poland seized the opportunity to invade our land. He triumphed over Count Vacek and the Vršovice family, leaving devastation in his wake across three districts in the Hradecko region. Count Vacek, bearing the weight of this calamity, assigned full blame to Mutina—an individual from the Vršovice family—for the entire disaster.

Svatopluk, consumed by anger, chose to believe Vacek's account and, driven by his wrath, vowed to obliterate Mutina and his entire lineage. However, to maintain the presence of the Vršovice family within his ranks, Svatopluk concealed his dreadful intentions, presenting them with a façade of goodwill.

Upon his arrival in Bohemia, a council convened at Vratislav Castle near Vysoké Mýto. Mutina, accompanied by his two young sons and other members of the Vršovice family, appeared unaware of any guilt. The duke positioned himself in their midst, delivering impassioned words that exposed Mutina's faithlessness, as well as the countless betrayals and crimes committed by his lineage. The present Vršovice members were swiftly condemned to death, and those who eliminated any absent family members were promised the entirety of their estate as a reward. Chroniclers recount a grim tally of nearly three thousand lives lost, sparing not even the innocent children. Two young boys were forcefully torn from their mother's embrace by heartless executioners, dragged to the market square, and mercilessly slain. As the sun dimmed its light, roses shed tears, and the world mourned the magnitude of such unfathomable fury.

In the wake of these events, the courageous Prince Svatopluk suffered the loss of an eye when a nimble branch pierced deep into it, necessitating its extraction. Undeterred, the following year he continued to lend his support to Henry V in the conflict against Boleslav the Wrymouth of Poland. Yet, as twilight descended upon the land, and Svatopluk returned to his encampment from the German army, tragedy struck. He was fatally pierced by a spear, succumbing to his wounds. Amid the ensuing chaos, the perpetrator, mounted upon a swift horse, managed to elude the deserved punishment. With this, the Vršovice lineage reached its final chapter.

Božetěch and Kosmas

During the reign of Vratislav, two remarkable individuals resided in Bohemia: Abbot Božetěch and Canon Kosmas.

Abbot Božetěch, the esteemed leader of Sázava Monastery, possessed exceptional skills as a painter, carver, and builder. His artistic talents extended beyond painting beautiful images, encompassing wood carving, stone cutting, and lathe work. Božetěch undertook the reconstruction of Sázava Monastery, the Sázava Church, and their surrounding structures, adorning them with exquisite craftsmanship and generously providing for all their needs. King Vratislav and many Czech nobles held him in high regard, appreciating his artistic prowess. However, alongside his many virtues, Božetěch also harbored excessive ambition, which led him astray on numerous occasions.

One such instance occurred during a grand religious ceremony in Prague Castle's St. Vitus Cathedral. Bishop Kosmas, either forgetting or unable to place the crown on King Vratislav's head during the mass, found himself at a loss. Sensing an opportunity, Abbot Božetěch, who enjoyed the king's favor, retrieved the crown from the altar and placed it upon the monarch's head. However, the bishop interpreted this act as a bold intrusion into his episcopal authority, resulting in his deep anger towards Božetěch. Determined to remove him from his position as abbot, the bishop persisted until numerous Czech nobles intervened on Božetěch's behalf. Eventually, the bishop imposed an extraordinary penance upon Božetěch as reparation for his transgression. He commanded the skilled artist, well-versed in sculpture and turning, to craft a wooden crucifix of his own height and width. Once completed, Božetěch was to carry this crucifix upon his own shoulders, traversing the arduous journey on foot to Rome and placing it within the grand church of St. Peter. Complying with the penance assigned to him, Abbot Božetěch humbly submitted himself to the task, diligently crafting a magnificent crucifix. Overcoming countless challenges, including the traversal of towering Alps, traversing German lands, and navigating Italian territories, he eventually reached Rome in 1090, fulfilling his penance by placing the beautifully carved crucifix in the main church of St. Peter.

Canon Kosmas was born in the year 1045, during the reign of Duke Břetislav I of Bohemia. He received his early education in Prague before embarking on a journey to the city of Liège in the Low Countries (present-day Belgium) to pursue various studies. At the age of 53, he was ordained as a priest and quickly rose to the position of canon and dean of the Prague chapter at St. Vitus Cathedral.

One of Canon Kosmas's most notable contributions was his comprehensive historical account of the Czech nation. He diligently chronicled his own personal experiences and knowledge acquired from others, providing invaluable insights into the history of our illustrious ancestors. We owe him a tremendous debt of gratitude for preserving this knowledge, as his work served as a source of inspiration for subsequent generations to continue documenting our rich heritage. Kosmas's reputation among our ancestors was one of great esteem, as he was known for his truthfulness, erudition, humility, and willingness to assist and protect anyone who sought his aid.

On October 21, 1125, at the honorable age of 80, during the reign of Duke Soběslav, Canon Kosmas passed away, leaving behind a legacy that was deeply mourned by all who knew him.

Duke Soběslav

In the year 1125, the Czechs elected Soběslav as their duke, recognizing his exceptional qualities as a ruler. Soběslav was a man of remarkable character, unaffected by either good fortune or adversity. He treated his subjects with kindness and generosity, showing loyalty, sincerity, and fairness to both Czech lords and foreigners alike. It was no wonder that the Czech people held him in deep affection.

However, the growing strength of the Czechs became a cause for concern for Lothar, the German king of that time. Lothar devised a plan to undermine Soběslav's position and impose a weaker duke upon the Czechs. He started by asserting that the Czechs had no right to choose their duke without the emperor's approval, and subsequently declared war against Soběslav.

Upon learning of the king's intentions, Duke Soběslav responded with brevity and humility, expressing his trust in God's mercy and the support of the revered saints Václav and Vojtěch. He traversed the land of Bohemia, seeking solace in churches, and encouraging his fellow countrymen to remain courageous in the face of the impending conflict.

In the year 1126, King Lothar instigated a war amidst the harsh winter season. With a formidable army, he crossed the Ore Mountains and advanced towards Duke Soběslav's position near Chlumec, by Teplice. The landscape featured a wide valley enclosed by towering mountains. As Soběslav, a seasoned and courageous warrior, surveyed the situation, he aimed to minimize unnecessary bloodshed.

In his wisdom, Soběslav dispatched messengers from the Czech lords to deliver a clear message to King Lothar. The message emphasized the long-standing tradition and law of the Czech nation, asserting that the selection of their duke was exclusively within the authority of Czech leaders, subject to the confirmation of the emperors. The messengers conveyed the sentiment that the Czechs were unwilling to bear additional burdens and would rather face a just battle even at the cost of their lives. They warned Lothar that if he persisted in his endeavor, God would be the ultimate judge between them.

Regrettably, King Lothar, driven by pride, refused to heed the counsel and instruction of the Czech messengers. He remained resolute in his position, unwilling to relent.

The decisive battle took place on February 18, where Duke Soběslav led his forces to a resounding victory. King Lothar, gripped by fear and witnessing the complete collapse of his forces, sought refuge on a nearby hill with those who remained loyal to him. However, the Czechs, relentless in their pursuit, closed in on his camp, sealing off any possible escape routes. Lothar found himself trapped, with no option but to seek peace.

In this moment of triumph, Soběslav held the power to impose harsh conditions on Lothar as part of the peace treaty. Yet, driven by his noble character and a recognition that his cause had been affirmed by God's judgment, he chose a different path. Displaying compassion towards the defeated king, Soběslav extended kindness rather than humiliation. In the spirit of reconciliation, he sought no retribution or demands that would further humiliate Lothar. Instead, he granted him the freedom to return home, releasing the captured Germans without seeking any ransom.

Remarkably, despite their earlier conflict, this act of magnanimity forged a lasting bond between Soběslav and Lothar. Their friendship blossomed and remained unbroken until their respective deaths, demonstrating the power of forgiveness and the capacity for reconciliation.

Vladislav II and the Holy Land

Duke Soběslav peacefully passed away in 1140, with unwavering trust in his Christian faith, in the town of Hostínhrad, known as Hostinné today. In response, the Czech lords assembled once again and proceeded to elect Vladislav II, the eldest son of Vladislav I, as the new duke. The installation of Vladislav II as the successor to Soběslav was marked by grand ceremonial proceedings, reflecting the power and courage that he possessed, which surpassed even that of his esteemed predecessor.

In 1147, Vladislav II actively participated in the Second Crusade. The Crusades stemmed from a longstanding grievance regarding the control of the sacred land where our Savior was born, taught, suffered, and ultimately died on the cross. This holy land was under the dominion of unbelievers, particularly the Turks, who held to the Muslim faith and showed contempt towards Christians. The faithful pilgrims who ventured to these lands endured immense suffering due to the malevolent actions of these Turks.

A pious hermit named Peter from France personally experienced the mistreatment inflicted by the Turks during his pilgrimage. He shared his grievances with the pope, who advised him to embark on a journey throughout Europe, spreading the message of the plight faced by Christians in the Holy Land. Peter diligently preached about his encounters and relayed the pope's call to arms against the merciless Turks. Stirred by his words, numerous Christians eagerly volunteered to march against these wicked oppressors and liberate the Holy Land from their grip.

They adorned their garments with the symbol of the cross, distinguishing themselves as Crusaders. These wars came to be known as the Crusades because these valiant individuals were driven by their fervent desire to fight and sacrifice their lives for the cross, representing Jesus Christ. The initial Crusade was undoubtedly blessed by God's grace. The Christians emerged victorious over the Turks, reclaiming Jerusalem and establishing a Christian kingdom. However, disputes and conflicts arose among the Christians themselves, leading to a decline in their hold on the region. The Turks regrouped, expelling Christians from numerous cities, attacking travelers, and subjecting them to various hardships.

Consequently, the pope issued a second call to Christians, urging them to take up arms against the Turks. In a manner reminiscent of Peter's earlier efforts, Saint Bernard embarked on a journey across various regions, rallying Christians to unite and combat the unbelievers. King Louis VII of France and Conrad III, the German king, pledged their forces to confront the Turks. Our own Vladislav, along with many Czech lords and common people, answered the call and joined the crusading armies.

Unfortunately, the journey to the Holy Land proved perilous, and countless Crusaders lost their lives along the way. Hunger claimed the lives of some, while others fell victim to Turkish attacks. It is said that only one in ten Crusaders reached their intended destination, with the remaining nine perishing on the arduous journey. Our beloved countrymen shared the same fate. They carried an ardent longing for the land where Jesus had walked and sacrificed, but tragically, many perished before reaching it. Vladislav experienced profound sorrow for his fellow Czechs, but recognizing the potential turmoil that could ensue in Bohemia, he made the difficult decision to return home. Though he would have willingly given his life in the holy battle, he understood the importance of stability in Bohemia. Only a handful of Czechs managed to reach the Holy Land, where they performed countless acts of heroism and valor.

Vladislav the Peaceful

Following Vladislav's demise in 1174, challenging times befell Bohemia. The Přemyslids, plagued by internal discord, found themselves engaged in near-constant conflict with one another. There is nothing more detrimental to a nation than civil war. As these clashes persisted, our beloved homeland teetered on the edge of ruin. Witnessing this dire state of affairs, the Czech people fervently prayed to the Lord God, beseeching Him to spare them from further calamity. It was precisely during this tumultuous period that Jindřich Břetislav, the Duke of Bohemia and also the Bishop of Prague, passed away in 1197.

In response, the Czech lords convened and elected Vladislav, the youngest son of the esteemed King Vladislav II, as the new duke. Just recently released from imprisonment, Vladislav's worthiness and benevolence were evident, prompting his selection as duke. Grateful for the kindness shown to him, Vladislav remained steadfast in his commitment to doing good wherever, whenever, and to whomever he could.

The welfare of the nation stood as his paramount concern. However, even within the country, there were those who harbored ill-will towards him, including his own elder brother, Přemysl Otakar, who, despite being a courageous and noble lord, held animosity towards Vladislav.

Otakar mustered an army, displaying formidable strength as he marched towards Prague with the intention of toppling his brother from the throne and seizing power for himself. However, Vladislav countered him with his noble character. Amassing an even larger army, Vladislav confronted Otakar, but instead of engaging in battle, he chose a different path, unwilling to shed innocent blood. He would have willingly sacrificed himself if it meant serving the greater good of the country. Secretly, Vladislav summoned his brother and feigned ambition for power, only to reveal his true intentions by saying, "Hasn't there been enough bloodshed between us, brothers? How long must our diligent people suffer?"

In a remarkable display of brotherly love, Vladislav and Otakar reconciled, setting aside their differences in pursuit of harmony. Vladislav willingly relinquished supreme power in Bohemia, moved by his noble brother's response. Embracing each other sincerely, they sought forgiveness and expressed their mutual desire to never deprive one another of their rightful domains.

The Czech lands were then divided between the two brothers. Přemysl Otakar assumed rule over Bohemia as the elder, while Vladislav reigned in Moravia as the younger. They pledged to support each other in the best interests of the country. This victory of brotherly harmony and love for the homeland was cause for celebration. Vladislav's unwavering loyalty to his elder brother until his death exemplified his noble soul. It is truly inspiring to witness Vladislav's actions, as he dedicated himself to strengthening and enhancing his brother's power, leaving behind a poignant example of brotherly love.

King Přemysl Otakar I

Přemysl Otakar I emerged as a wise and formidable ruler during a time when our homeland was often overlooked by neighboring nations. The once-glorious name of the Czechs had faded from the consciousness of foreign lands, and the internal discord among the Přemyslids was to blame for this unfortunate decline. It became evident that German kings used the disputes within the Přemyslid dynasty to assert their authority and impose their will upon the Czech lands, which proved detrimental to our realm.

However, Přemysl Otakar had a clear vision: to safeguard the independence and autonomy of Bohemia and restore its former glory. He seized a crucial opportunity to achieve this goal soon after assuming power. Following the death of Frederick I, a power struggle erupted among the electors in Germany over the selection of a new king. Some supported Philip, the Duke of Swabia and a relative of the previous German kings, while others favored Otto from the ducal house of Saxony. In the end, both were elected, with neither willing to yield to the other.

Realizing the fragmented state of German affairs, Přemysl Otakar saw an opening to advance the interests of Bohemia. He skillfully navigated the complex political landscape and capitalized on the divided German kingship. Through strategic alliances and diplomatic maneuvers, he worked tirelessly to secure the sovereignty and reputation of our beloved land. His astute actions set the stage for Bohemia's resurgence on the international stage, ensuring that our nation would no longer be overlooked or overshadowed.

Přemysl Otakar I vividly remembered how the German kings had historically exploited the discord within the Přemyslid dynasty to enhance their own power and prestige. With similar unfavorable circumstances unfolding in Germany, Přemysl saw an opportunity to secure benefits for his state and nation. As a German elector, he aligned himself with Philip of Swabia, but not without certain conditions. Přemysl demanded three key assurances from Philip: firstly, the affirmation that no German king would interfere in the election of Bohemian rulers; secondly, the direct subordination of every Prague bishop to the Czech ruler, rather than being subject to the German king; and finally, the recognition of every Czech ruler as a king. Although Přemysl Otakar was crowned during a military campaign in

Germany, the inheritance of this title, like Vratislav II and Vladislav II before him, still required confirmation by the pope, as was customary at the time.

Notably, as the then pope, Innocent III, showed favor towards Otto of Saxony rather than Philip of Swabia, Přemysl made the strategic decision to switch allegiance and support Otto. Fortunately, Otto agreed to honor the previous negotiations between Přemysl and Philip. Moreover, in 1204, the pope officially confirmed the royal status of Bohemia for all eternity. Hence, we recognize Přemysl Otakar I as the first hereditary king of Bohemia, distinguishing him from Vratislav II and Vladislav II, who held the title of personal kings. This pivotal moment solidified the enduring legacy of the Přemyslid dynasty and the elevated status of the Bohemian monarchy.

As the Czech king, Přemysl Otakar, along with his noble brother Vladislav, the Margrave of Moravia, dedicated themselves wholeheartedly to the improvement of the Czech realm. They embarked on ambitious endeavors, constructing roads, fostering economic growth, establishing new towns and villages, and prioritizing the welfare of their subjects. Their efforts yielded remarkable results— trade and craftsmanship thrived, the country flourished, and an atmosphere of liveliness and joy permeated throughout.

Yet, Přemysl Otakar I made certain decisions that had adverse consequences for the Czech nation. One such misstep involved the influx of foreigners into Bohemia, granting them privileges and rights that even native Czechs did not possess to the same extent. Although his reign brought about progress and prosperity, these actions created a sense of imbalance and inequality among the people.

In his pursuit of stability and to prevent the bloody conflicts that traditionally plagued the succession of Czech rulers, Přemysl Otakar introduced a special law that transformed the system of succession. No longer would the eldest member of the Přemyslid dynasty automatically ascend to the throne, as dictated by the Law of Seniority established by Břetislav. Instead, it would be the firstborn or oldest son of each king who would inherit the crown. As a testament to this new law, Přemysl Otakar's oldest son, Václav, was crowned and acknowledged as the future king of Bohemia while his father was still alive. This momentous occasion took place in 1228 at Prague Castle, amidst grandeur and splendor. From that point forward, Přemysl Otakar ruled alongside his son until his passing on December 15, 1230, when he was called to the eternal realm by God.

Přemysl Otakar I's reign left a lasting legacy as a wise and influential ruler who tirelessly pursued the independence and prosperity of Bohemia. His efforts to establish the autonomy of the Czech lands and secure the royal dignity reinstated the illustrious reputation of the Czechs and elevated their standing among other nations. While some of his actions may have caused harm, his unwavering commitment to the well-being of his subjects and the advancement of the realm remains a testament to his rule. Přemysl Otakar I continues to be remembered as a symbol of a strong and enlightened leader in the annals of Czech history.

King Václav

King Václav, the eldest son of Přemysl Otakar, emerged as a formidable ruler. His court in Prague exuded grandeur, and his reputation extended far and wide. The people held him in high regard, while his adversaries quivered in fear.

During the initial years of his reign, the Czech lands experienced an era of unprecedented peace. Václav capitalized on this tranquility to enhance and uplift his realm. A patron of the arts and sciences, he welcomed and esteemed learned individuals at his court. The number of schools multiplied under his reign, offering opportunities for people to acquire knowledge and education. In those times, the ability to read and write was a rarity. You, dear children, are fortunate to have access to education from a tender age!

King Václav fostered the popularity of various knightly festivities in Bohemia. Knights gathered on designated days, engaging in spirited celebrations and engaging in combat to vie for victory. The triumphant knight would receive a well-deserved reward.

The wealth of Bohemia flourished under Václav's rule. The land abounded in precious metals, fertile grain, and all manner of essential resources. Václav's extraordinary generosity and philanthropy extended to the less fortunate, as he provided ample support for the poor. He established numerous monasteries and lavished them with endowments. Furthermore, he invited settlers, miners, skilled craftsmen, and diverse artists from Germany to take residence in these monasteries and towns. Their presence served to enrich Czech society by imparting various crafts and customs. However, a misstep was made when he granted significant privileges and rights to these foreigners, burdening the native artisans. Nonetheless, the Czech towns thrived, and to facilitate seamless communication between them, new roads were constructed.

The influx of Germans into Bohemia also had its consequences, as Czechs adopted German customs, attire, and more. However, this was not always advantageous. It is important for every nation to preserve and honor the beauty and nobility of its own heritage. Unfortunately, at that time, the allure of novelty prevailed, and changes spread rapidly throughout the country, transforming its very essence. Regrettably, even the German language gained influence and predominance at the royal court, with King Václav himself composing German songs.

Another notable development during this period was the introduction of surnames in Bohemia. Previously, sons did not bear the same name as their fathers. However, the introduction of surnames initially leaned heavily towards German names, reflecting the prevailing fashion. Even the nobility started giving their castles German names. Some older and wiser Czechs expressed their disapproval, lamenting the deterioration of their time-honored traditions. Yet, fashion held its sway.

In the midst of these changes, Kutná Hora's mines began yielding substantial profits, and trade experienced a surge. The Czech people found themselves engaging more extensively with foreign nations, leading to some beneficial and positive outcomes.

One of King Václav's most cherished pastimes was hunting. He frequently embarked on extensive hunts in the vast Bohemian forests, which were considerably larger in those days. It was during one such hunt that he suffered a mishap, as a swift branch struck his eye, resulting in the loss of one eye. Consequently, many affectionately referred to him as "One-Eyed."

Brave Jaroslav

In the past, the Mongolian people resided in eastern Asia. Known also as the Tatars, they were a fierce and ruthless nation characterized by their nomadic lifestyle. Unlike settled civilizations, the Mongols continuously migrated from one place to another. In the 13th century, they witnessed a significant expansion of their empire under the leadership of Genghis Khan. Following Genghis Khan's demise, his son Ogedei was elected as the ruler or khan of the Tatars. Under his command, they embarked on a conquest of Asia, eventually venturing into Europe.

The Mongols swept across the Russian Empire, leaving a trail of devastation in their wake. They ravaged Poland and Hungary before setting their sights on Silesia. In Silesia, they launched a destructive campaign that included the burning of the great city of Wroclaw and the merciless killing of numerous individuals. Duke Henry II of Wroclaw valiantly opposed them near the city of Legnica, but tragically, he was slain, and his army suffered defeat in the spring of 1241. Horrifying tales about the Tatars quickly circulated in the western regions, instilling fear and panic among the populace. People abandoned their cities and villages, seeking refuge in the safety of forests, where they concealed themselves in caves and other hiding places to evade the savage Tatar invaders.

King Václav I held grave concerns about the potential invasion of the Tatars into his kingdom. To safeguard Bohemia, he embarked on a journey throughout the land, overseeing the fortification of castles and cities while ensuring their ample provisioning. He took decisive action by barricading and securing the northeastern passages, which the Tatars intended to use for their incursion. These passages were now guarded by strong troops. No sooner had these measures been implemented than news arrived of the Tatars approaching the Czech border. Despite their proximity, they failed to breach Bohemia's defenses.

Redirecting their attention to Moravia, the Tatars descended upon it like an ominous cloud. Promptly informed of this development, King Václav wasted no time in dispatching the valiant Czech lord Jaroslav from Slivno[7] with an army to Moravia.

---

[7] Indeed, it is true that Jaroslav belonged to that family, which later adopted the star in their coat of arms and

Jaroslav swiftly secured strategic locations such as Brno and other fortified cities, stationing garrisons to protect them. He then hastened to Olomouc, where approximately 4,000 armed Moravians joined his forces, bolstering the warrior count to approximately 12,000 within the city walls. Meanwhile, the Tatars left a trail of destruction in their wake, burning villages, sacking cities, and inflicting harm upon the populace.

Reports depicted the Moravians falling like blades of grass before the swift swords of the Tatars, akin to reapers in a field. Eventually, the Tatars laid siege to Olomouc, defended by the indomitable Jaroslav. Fierce attacks were launched against the city, but the Moravians valiantly resisted and repelled their assailants. This intense struggle persisted for a prolonged period.

On a fateful day in late June 1241, bands of marauding Tartars roamed across Moravia, pillaging and wreaking havoc. Jaroslav, well aware of their movements, swiftly rallied his warriors and summoned them to the church. There, amidst solemn prayers, a holy mass was conducted, and every soldier received communion, preparing themselves for the impending battle. As the divine service concluded, they stealthily departed from

---

the name Šternberk, and from whom the current counts of Šternberk descend.

Olomouc, venturing forth to ambush the unsuspecting Tartars who were caught in slumber. A fierce and bloody clash ensued, with Jaroslav himself leading the charge. Through his unwavering bravery, he fought his way to the Tartar chieftain, delivering a fatal blow with his sword. The demise of their leader struck terror into the hearts of the Tartars, who hastily fled from the lands of Moravia.

A poignant account of this historic battle was preserved by an unknown poet from the Old Czech era, immortalized within the pages of the revered Královedvorský manuscript. The concluding excerpt of this poem, translated into modern Czech, resonates as follows:

As armies advance, a majestic sight unfolds,
From distant lands they gather, a story to be told.
With swords of weight, by their sides they sway,
Shields upon their shoulders, gleaming in array.
Helmets adorn their heads, vibrant and bold,
Beneath them, horses dance, their spirits untold.
The melodies of forest horns fill the air,
Drums resound, announcing the battle's flare.

Swiftly we clash, like clouds in a storm,
A mist rises, as dust takes its form.
Swords clash and arrows hiss through the air,
Spears snap, lances clamor, creating a fervent affair.

It is a dance of valor, a symphony of might,
Amidst chaos and destruction, we fight.

Blood flows like rain, a river of red,
Corpses lie like fallen trees, their fate now shed.
Heads split in two, arms severed in strife,
As warriors pierce their foes, with fierce and fiery
life.

Roars and cries echo, carried by the wind,
As Christians retreat, the Tatars' pursuit begins.
But behold, Jaroslav descends with grace,
A noble eagle, his presence we embrace.
With steel-clad shoulders, a symbol of might,
Courage beneath, valor shining bright.
His helmet bears a resounding reputation,
A warrior's spirit, a force of creation.

With unwavering determination, he charges ahead,
Like a lion provoked, his instincts widespread.
Guided by warm blood, his gaze set on prey,
He hunts with purpose, unyielding in his way.
The Czechs follow, like a hailstorm's might,
United against Tatars, they join the fight.
With force, Jaroslav confronts the Kublajevis'
horde,

A clash of spears, a mighty crack, their clash
adored.

Drenched in blood, a warrior untamed,
Jaroslav impales his foe, honor regained.
From shoulder to hip, the Tatar falls,
Among the fallen, lifeless in death's calls.
A quiver and bow rattles above, in solemn refrain,
The entire Tatar host trembles in fear's domain.
Discarding their spears, they flee from the light,
Seeking refuge where the sun shines bright.

Thus, Haná is liberated, from Tatar's cruel might,
Jaroslav's valorous feat, a beacon of resplendent
light.

In poetic dance, a tale of bravery's course,
Where heroes rise, with valor as their source.

In such fashion, the united forces of the Czechs and Moravians successfully repelled the formidable Tartar nation, whose mere presence sent tremors throughout Europe. In recognition of his unwavering bravery and pivotal role in this triumph, the king, filled with gratitude, bestowed upon the gallant Jaroslav vast estates in the lands of Moravia. It was there that he erected a majestic castle, forever etching his name in our collective memory. That castle is none other than Šternberk, proudly situated on the left bank of the Morava River, near the city of Olomouc. Its imposing presence stands as a testament to the valorous deeds of Jaroslav and serves as a symbol of our enduring history.

Přemysl Otakar II

The Czech kingdom reached the zenith of its power, glory, and renown under the reign of Přemysl Otakar II, the illustrious son of Václav I. This exceptional ruler expanded the boundaries of the Czech realm by incorporating numerous new territories.

In 1246, the renowned Babenberg dynasty, ruling over Austria and Styria, came to an end. Seizing this opportunity, certain Austrian estates appealed to the Czech ruler, Přemysl Otakar, urging him to assume control over the vacant lands. Meanwhile, Bela IV, the King of Hungary, took hold of Styria and demanded that Otakar relinquish the Austrian territories to him. However, Přemysl Otakar staunchly refused, defeated Bela in battle, and compelled him to surrender the southwestern portion of Styria.

Shortly thereafter, dissatisfied Styrian lords approached Otakar seeking his aid against Bela, whom they accused of oppressing them. Responding to their plea, Otakar assembled a formidable army and marched against Bela. Nevertheless, Bela countered with an even larger force to confront him.

Their decisive clash occurred at the confluence of the Morava River and the Danube, where bravery resonated on both sides. Ultimately, the Czechs emerged triumphant, pushing the Hungarians deep into their own territory. Realizing the futility of further resistance, Bela sued for peace, requesting to retain control over the entirety of Styria.

Thus, it came to pass in 1260. In celebration of this resounding victory, King Otakar established the town of Marchek in Austria, near the Morava River, as a lasting testament to the Czech triumph.

Shortly after, in 1260, Duke Oldřich, who held dominion over Carinthia and Carniola, passed away, and he bequeathed these lands to King Otakar. As a result, the Czech realm expanded from the Krkonoše Mountains nearly to the Adriatic Sea. While the Czech and Moravian lands were under the direct rule of the Czech king, with no higher authority, Otakar governed Austria, Styria, Carinthia, and Carniola as a vassal prince to the German kings. However, these kings did not command much respect in Germany during that time, rendering them weak and posing no significant obstacle to Přemysl Otakar.

Prior to this, Otakar had embarked on campaigns in Prussia to spread the Christian faith among the local pagans. He achieved numerous victories and founded the city of Kralovec, situated not far from the sea. Hence, it could be said that the Czech realm extended almost from one sea to another, encompassing both the Baltic Sea and the Adriatic Sea. Otakar's glory was immense; he commanded the utmost respect from all, and he feared no one. The Tatars dubbed him the Iron King due to his invincible, iron-clad army, while other nations referred to him as the Golden King because of the grandeur of his court and his remarkable generosity.

During this period, prosperity abounded in Bohemia. Otakar established many towns, prioritized the well-being of his subjects, and took measures to ensure their safety. He implemented a division of the land into counties and established new and improved offices. The Czech land was enriched with precious metals, gold, and silver. It yielded plentiful crops and supported thriving livestock. Trade and industry flourished, bringing widespread joy. It is unfortunate that this period of prosperity did not endure for a longer time!

Fall of the Přemysl Empire

Sadly, during that time in the German Empire, a culture of might prevailing over right had taken hold, with the strong oppressing the weak. The German princes, determined to bring an end to this injustice, elected Rudolf, Count of Habsburg, as their king.

However, in order for Rudolf to gain the support of the German princes, he had to promise to reclaim all the lands that Přemysl Otakar had recently added to the Czech realm. Upon learning of this, Otakar refused to recognize Rudolf as the German king, leading to a war. Some Czech lords, disapproving of Otakar's disorder, decided to abandon their king and join Rudolf's cause.

Consequently, Přemysl Otakar was forced to humble himself before Rudolf and acknowledge him as the German king. Rudolf took control of Austria, Styria, Carinthia, and Carniola, leaving only Bohemia and Moravia under Otakar's rule (in 1276). The plan was to achieve complete reconciliation between Rudolf and Přemysl Otakar through strategic marriages between their offspring and other agreed-upon compensations.

However, when Rudolf presented excessive demands to Otakar, the latter rebelled against him. The two forces clashed in a momentous battle near the town of Marchek, which Otakar himself had founded. Despite being vastly outnumbered, with Rudolf commanding over a hundred thousand well-trained soldiers while Otakar had only twenty-six thousand inexperienced recruits, the Czechs emerged victorious.

Then, Otakar summoned Milota of Dědice to lead the Moravians into battle against the remaining German forces. However, treacherous Milota betrayed them all, shouting, "The battle is lost! Save yourselves by fleeing!" Many others followed his lead and fled, abandoning the fight. But Přemysl Otakar refused to run away. He chose to stay and face the consequences, even if it meant his own demise. He fought valiantly, refusing to witness the defeat of his Czech brethren. Despite sustaining seventeen wounds, he continued to fight until, at last, he fell and lost his life near Suchá Krutá (Dürrenkrut).

When Rudolf caught sight of Otakar's lifeless body, he was overcome with sorrow. He wept as he gazed upon the renowned king, now motionless and covered in dust and blood. This tragic event occurred on August 26th, 1278.

The glorious empire of Otakar was brought to ruin!

Our poet, Vincenc Furch, mournfully sings of this battle:

On the day of Saint Rufus,
on the Moravian field,
Czech blood flowed in torrents,
turning the earth crimson.

There stood the Czech troops,
led by Otakar;
Oh glorious, golden king,
this was your final fight!

King Otakar the victorious,
whose name was known beyond the Czech lands,
reaching to the Baltic Sea,
fell by his Morava.

The Morava mourns in darkness,
and the people weep,
as if the last ray of sun
has vanished from the land.

Original Czech:

Na den svatého Rufa
na poli Moravském
krev česká tekla proudem,
až zrůžověla zem.

Tam české pluky stály,
Otakar vedl voj:
Ó, slavný, zlatý králi!

to poslední tvůj boj.

Král Otakar vítězný,
jenž jméno české nes'
až k moři Baltickému,
u své Moravy kles'.

Morava hučí temně,
i pláče všechen lid,
tak jak by v zemi zhynul
poslední slunce svit.

Tragic Times

Great King Přemysl Otakar II had a sole heir, his son Václav, who was just seven years old when his father passed away. Unfortunately, the regency of the Czech lands fell into the hands of Otakar's avaricious uncle, Otto, the Margrave of Brandenburg.

Under Otto's rule, Bohemia plunged into a sorrowful state. He viewed everything in the kingdom as his own possession, taking money from merchants, looting treasures from churches, and transferring them to his own domain. He even lacked compassion for the deceased, desecrating graves to seize any precious gold and silver items he could find. His soldiers were equally ruthless, confiscating livestock and crops from peasants, seizing footwear and clothing from townsfolk, and sparing no one, not even the destitute.

Young Václav faced countless trials under the grip of the greedy Otto. At the tender age of eight, he and his mother were imprisoned within the walls of Bezděz Castle. Although the queen managed to escape, young Václav remained captive. Otto banished him to a foreign land, likely the town of Žitava in Lusatia. There, the poor child wandered, clad in tattered garments and worn-out shoes, enduring hunger and bitter cold.

Meanwhile, the land of Bohemia endured immense suffering. Famine plagued the region, and devastating epidemics ravaged the population, causing countless deaths from hunger and plague. Chroniclers of that era vividly depicted the harrowing distress. Desperate circumstances drove some to unthinkable measures, with accounts suggesting that the impoverished resorted to consuming corpses in their desperation. Many succumbed to disease and starvation. In the span of a single year, a fifth of the Czech population perished, succumbing to the dire circumstances.

Eventually, mercy shone upon our beleaguered homeland, as a bountiful harvest arrived, providing much-needed relief. Otto, the cause of much hardship, departed from Bohemia, leaving the administration of the land in the hands of Bishop Eberhard, hailing from Brandenburg. News of the wealth and treasures in Bohemia spread, drawing a wave of German opportunists who mercilessly tormented the fleeing populace seeking refuge in the mountains and forests. These audacious interlopers shamelessly pillaged our land. In response, some Czech lords, unable to bear the torment any longer, rose up and ruthlessly struck down the invaders wherever they found them. In this tumultuous period, German King Rudolf intervened, seeking to broker a compromise between the warring factions.

Meanwhile, young Václav reached the age of twelve, prompting the Czechs to write to Otto, demanding the return of their prince so they could crown him king. However, Otto stubbornly refused unless they paid him a hefty sum of fifteen thousand hřivnas of silver, claiming it was payment for his services in raising the young prince. Determined to secure Václav's freedom, the Czechs scraped together the funds to meet Otto's demand, hoping to rid themselves of him and his entourage. Yet, Otto's greed knew no bounds, and he demanded an additional twenty thousand hřivnas. The Czechs found themselves unable to meet this exorbitant demand, but they had no choice. They pledged several towns and castles to Otto in exchange for the release of young Václav. The Czechs rejoiced, eagerly awaiting his arrival. They gathered in great numbers to welcome him and, together, made their way to St. Vitus Cathedral, offering prayers to the Lord God, beseeching Him to bestow happiness and glory upon their young king.

Václav II

The Czechs found themselves blessed once again as the Lord God showered them with favorable times. In the face of suffering and adversity, it is crucial to remember that the sun always rises after it sets.

Václav proved to be an exemplary leader, exceeding the expectations of his people. He prioritized education, acquiring the ability to read and write, earning him a place among the most erudite kings of Bohemia. Kind, devout, and just, Václav II governed with a conscientious approach, seeking the counsel of wise and knowledgeable individuals to guide his decisions and uplift the prosperity of his subjects.

Consequently, the Czechs held him in high regard, while foreigners readily acknowledged his authority. The Duchy of Opole, Kraków, and Sandomierz willingly submitted to his rule. The Poles chose him as their king, and in 1300, he received the crown of Poland in a coronation ceremony held in Gniezno. Not long after, the

Hungarians approached him, extending an offer for the Hungarian crown. However, Václav declined, recognizing the weight of bearing three crowns on a single head. In response, the Hungarians proposed that his son, also named Václav, assume the Hungarian throne. Václav agreed to this arrangement, but it sparked envy from Pope Boniface and King Albert, the son of the late King Rudolf.

Albert's futile military campaign against the prosperous Václav ended in defeat, forcing him to retreat in disappointment. No other king in Europe possessed as much wealth in gold and silver as King Václav. He stood as the wealthiest monarch on the continent. Václav minted exquisite silver coins, renowned as Prague groschen, which were stacked and counted. Sixty Prague groschen formed one stack, equivalent to a silver hřivna. A groschen consisted of twelve coins. Czech coins were held in high esteem across all nations due to their purity and weight. Václav spared no effort in bringing honor to his country and raising the reputation of the Czech people.

The Kutná Hora mines yielded an unprecedented amount of silver. Václav's coronation in 1197 brought unparalleled grandeur to both nearby and distant lands. Contemporary historians recall that not even the court of Solomon had witnessed such magnificence. The city of Prague overflowed with domestic and foreign dignitaries, necessitating the erection of tents and buildings beyond its limits. A staggering 191,000 horses were provisioned for the royal expenses. A grand wooden palace was erected at the present-day location of Oujezd Prague, serving as the focal point of the coronation festivities. The coronation itself took place on the day of Pentecost. The royal attire consisted entirely of golden scales, adorned with precious stones of immeasurable value. For four days, the entire population was treated generously at the king's expense. Wine flowed freely from the fountains in the square of St. Gallus, and the city shimmered under the glow of large torches at night to ensure uninterrupted revelry. Prague's houses were bedecked with carpets and draperies, adding to the splendor of the occasion.

To the profound sorrow of our nation, Václav's life was cut short at the premature age of 34 in 1305. He found his resting place in Zbraslav Monastery near Prague, a testament to his own establishment.

Death of the Přemyslid Dynasty

Václav III ascended the throne at the tender age of sixteen, adorned with the three crowns of Czechia, Poland, and Hungary. Initially, he possessed both youth and comeliness, and his father's wise instructions lingered in his mind. However, the pernicious influence of his Hungarian advisors corrupted him swiftly, stifling his father's counsel. Henceforth, Václav's sole pursuits revolved around drinking and gambling. He recklessly squandered the vast lands his father had acquired for the Czech crown, lavishing wealth upon sycophants and companions whose loyalty proved transient. Regrettably, a sense of remorse only struck him when sobriety settled in, but by then, it was too late.

During a solemn visit to his father's resting place, Václav dared to engage in a heartfelt conversation. Revered Abbot Konrád of Zbraslav, a trusted advisor who had faithfully served his father, seized the opportunity to earnestly remind him of his responsibilities. This encounter touched Václav's heart genuinely, prompting him to renounce excessive indulgence and distance himself from immoral comrades who had led him astray. A glimmer of hope emerged, suggesting the possibility of a complete transformation.

In the face of a rebellion led by Vladislaus the Elbow-high in Poland, Václav III mustered an army and personally led the charge against him. Assembling in Olomouc, where troops from across the Czech lands gathered, Václav took up residence in the dean's house. Seeking respite from the scorching heat, he stepped out on a sweltering August 4th, 1306, attired in light garments. In a sudden and unexpected turn of events, a knight emerged, brandishing a drawn sword, and ruthlessly struck down Václav. The assailant made a hasty attempt to escape, but the guards swiftly apprehended him, tearing him apart. Identified as Sir Konrád of Botenštejn, originally from Dürnk, it was evident that he had been hired by someone to commit the murder.

With the demise of Václav III, the time-honored Slavic Přemyslid dynasty, which had reigned over Bohemia for six centuries, met its end by the sword. This illustrious lineage had produced thirty-two ruling princes and seven Czech kings. The extinction of this dynasty inflicted a profound misfortune upon Bohemia, yielding the lamentable consequence of the dissolution of the grand Slavic realm, forged through the union of Bohemia and Poland under a single sovereign, King Václav II.

Undoubtedly, this tragic conclusion could have been averted had Václav III diligently attended to his rule and dutifully safeguarded the inheritance bestowed upon him by his esteemed father from the very onset. It serves as a poignant reminder of the repercussions that arise from a life frequently led astray and unrestrained. For he who wields the whip often shall bear its scent, And one who keeps company with the wicked risks being tainted.

Elizabeth of Přemyslid

According to the accounts of Dalimil, an esteemed Czech historian, it is believed that Emperor Albert orchestrated the assassination of Václav III to secure his own family's ascension to the Czech throne. Yet, as the saying goes, ill-gotten wealth seldom endures beyond three generations, and history swiftly validated this proverb once again.

Pressured by circumstances, the Czechs found themselves compelled to select Rudolf, Albert's eldest son, as their king. Rudolf, who had to wed Elizabeth of Poland, the widow of Václav II, held the throne for a mere few months before his untimely demise. Determined not to be dictated to any longer, the Czechs took matters into their own hands and chose Henry of Carinthia as their sovereign. Henry, who had married Anna, the eldest daughter of King Václav II, failed to gain Albert's favor. Preparing for an impending war with the Czechs, Albert's ambitions were abruptly halted as he fell victim to assassination at the hands of his own cousin.

However, the Czechs found their discontent growing under Henry of Carinthia's rule, as his capabilities as a leader proved lacking. He introduced a multitude of foreign mercenaries into our nation, evoking painful memories of the despised Brandenburgers' reign. It became apparent to the Czech people that a more deserving ruler was needed.

Václav II, during his reign, had four daughters: Anna, Elizabeth, Margaret, and Agnes. Now, the attention of the Czechs turned towards the second daughter, who had spent her youth under her sister's care, immersing herself in decorative and artistic pursuits typically associated with women. Abbot Konrád of Zbraslav praised her talents, stating, "She did not idle away her time, but with her skilled hands, she crafts magnificent creations from gold, silver, pearls, and precious stones, bringing glory to God and enhancing human beauty. Through her virtue, even the most insignificant things become significant; her virgin hand produces remarkable ornaments."

Aware of Elizabeth's esteemed reputation among the Czechs, Henry sought to arrange her marriage to a lesser-ranked foreigner. However, his attempts failed, leading him to resort to dishonorable methods. This serves as a reminder of how ambition and unchecked desires can smother noble human sentiments.

To Elizabeth's misfortune, her own sister, Anna, spread malicious rumors about her, and there were even attempts to poison her. Yet, Elizabeth, guided by divine protection, remained unharmed, as God shielded her from harm.

Once, Jan of Stráž, a loyal friend of Elizabeth, received information about a secret plan to transport her far away from the court and hold her captive. Jan of Stráž wasted no time and, under the cover of night, escaped with the royal daughter to the town of Nymburk nad Labem. The townspeople received the princess with immense joy and ensured her safety, shielding her from any potential harm.

This event serves as a testament to the workings of divine justice, where sinners face the consequences of their actions. Soon after, the Czechs sent a message to Henry VII, who was originally the Count and Lord of Luxembourg and had been elected Emperor following Albert's reign and crowned in Rome. They requested that his son, Jan, be appointed as their king. Jan had already become engaged to Elizabeth. The Emperor agreed to their request, and preparations for the royal wedding commenced in Bohemia.

On August 14, 1310, the people of Prague opened the gate, which had been guarded by Henry's mercenaries. Elizabeth, who was already in Prague, embarked on a grand journey with her retinue to the imperial court in the city of Speyer. The wedding ceremony took place a few days later, and the newlyweds returned to Bohemia amidst great celebration. The dishonorable Henry of Carinthia, ousted from Prague Castle, had to flee the country under the cover of darkness. Anna, his wife, who had acted insensitively towards her sister, passed away on December 3 of the same year.

Jan of Luxembourg

Jan of Luxembourg was a king known for his prowess in warfare. Whenever the trumpets of war resounded and the clash of swords echoed, Jan would eagerly rush to the scene like a valiant knight, wielding his powerful sword that was welcomed everywhere. People of that era believed that no war could be successfully concluded without the assistance of the Lord God and the Czech king. Jan, however, paid little attention to the affairs of the Czech lands as long as there were funds for military expeditions. But when the coffers ran dry, he always turned his attention back to his homeland. Upon his return, he would gather several thousand hřivnas through fair or questionable means and set off on new campaigns and tournaments. No previous Czech king had traveled through as many foreign lands as he did. King Jan would spend the majority of spring and late autumn on horseback, journeying from one end of Europe to the other.

He embarked on three expeditions to distant Lithuania, located near the Baltic Sea. The inhabitants of that land faced persecution, and Jan aimed to convert them to the Christian faith. However, these expeditions did not yield the desired outcomes. Moreover, during the second campaign, Jan lost one eye, and due to inadequate treatment, he soon lost the other, becoming a blind king.

Meanwhile, as the Queen of Bohemia, Eliška led an unhappy life. Jan paid little attention to her, leaving her to live as a neglected widow. She found some solace during her time in Bavaria, but eventually returned to Prague, where she was joyfully welcomed. Upon her passing, the Czechs laid her to rest in the Zbraslav Monastery next to her father.

Once, Jan found himself in Tyrol when he received an invitation from the Italian city of Brescia. The city sought his protection and dominion over its territory in 1331. At that time, the Italian cities were embroiled in internal conflicts and wars. Jan, with his army, entered Italy and was warmly embraced by the people of Brescia. He displayed wise and decisive leadership, inspiring other cities to follow Brescia's example and submit to his rule. Even the proud city of Milan yielded to the power of the Czech king. However, these achievements drew the ire of Jan's neighboring rulers. Nevertheless, Jan remained resolute and undaunted. He was a true hero, and warfare was his domain. Unwilling to reconcile with his enemies, he declared, "In the name of the Lord! The more enemies we have, the greater spoils we shall acquire. I swear to God that whoever dares to face me first, I will vanquish them to such an extent that others will be frightened." This proclamation proved true when the Polish king, defeated and besieged by the Czechs in Krakow, sought peace, followed by others who acknowledged Jan's power.

Thus, Jan's bravery averted great danger to the Czech lands, not only shining a brighter light upon the glory of the Czech nation, but also expanding the kingdom, particularly through the victory over Polish King Vladislav Lokýtek, which resulted in the permanent annexation of Silesia. However, the control over Wallachian cities came to an end during this period.

During his journeys, Jan always rode the swiftest horses. An ancient chronicler shares an anecdote about him. Once, while traveling ahead of his entourage, he came across a wagoner who had become stuck in the mud with his wagon. The wagoner, not recognizing the king, pleaded for his horses to be used to pull the wagon. Jan granted his request and even personally encouraged the horses to free the wagon. When the wagon was safely on dry ground and the wagoner returned the horses to the king, he laughed and said, "Fool, do you think the king would ride a workhorse? Even if you offered a hundred hřivnas for it!" The wagoner indeed sold that horse in the nearest town for twenty hřivnas, which was quite a high price, equivalent to over 400 gold coins in our currency at the time.

While foreigners praised King Jan for his generosity and magnanimity, the Czech people viewed it more as extravagance, which they bore heavily. Jan seemed to consider the Czech lands merely as a source of wealth.

Death of King Jan

During that period, a brutal war raged between the French and the English. King Edward III of England sought to conquer the entire Kingdom of France, claiming his right to it as the son of a French princess. On the other hand, our valiant Jan had ties of kinship and friendship with King Philip of France. His second wife was a French princess, and his sister was married to the late French King. Jan enjoyed joyful moments in extravagant tournaments and festivities at the royal court in Paris. How could he not support his French allies?

Despite his blindness, Jan hurried to France and joined the French army to fight against the English. The battleground was set at Crecy in northern France, not far from the coast.

Brave Jan carefully assessed the enemy's position and the terrain, realizing that the English army held a significant advantage. He foresaw an unfavorable outcome and advised against engaging in battle. However, the French leaders ignored the advice of this seasoned warrior. The battle commenced, and the French forces suffered a crushing defeat. Amid the chaotic retreat, Czech soldiers implored the king to leave the field and protect his life. Yet, Jan declared, "The King of Bohemia will not flee from this battle. Today, I will either triumph or meet a glorious death. Lead me into the heart of the fight!" The Czech knights fastened the king's horse to their own and guided him into the thick of the battle. It was there, struck by numerous blows, that the blind hero met his demise.

Surrounded by fallen Czech heroes, Jan stood resolute, while his son Karel, gravely injured, had to be carried away from the battlefield. Jan's bravery commanded respect from both friend and foe. As the English king caught sight of his lifeless body, he wiped away tears and uttered, "Today, the epitome of chivalry has fallen. There has never been anyone in the world like this King of Bohemia!" With reverence, he plucked three ostrich feathers from Jan's helmet and presented them to his son, the renowned Black Prince, who emerged victorious that day. The Black Prince embraced the feathers, incorporating them into his shield alongside the king's motto, "Ich dien" (I serve). To this day, the motto adorns the shields of Welsh princes[8], a lasting tribute to our blind hero.

---

[8] Every English Crown Prince has the title of Prince of Wales.

Father of the Homeland

The adventurous King Jan had a son named Václav. At the age of seven, he was sent to the court of his French relatives for his education. He had access to exceptional teachers, unavailable in our country at the time. Diligent Václav not only excelled in age but also in wisdom, so much so that by the age of fifteen, he was considered one of the most educated youths. Suddenly, his father summoned him to Italy, where he aimed to establish a powerful domain. The inexperienced young man, who abhorred bloodshed, found himself leading an army entrusted with maintaining control over Italian cities. Surprisingly, he fulfilled this task admirably!

When King Jan relinquished his dominion in Italy, his son returned to his homeland. However, what a reunion it was with the people! Having spent time in a distant foreign land, he had forgotten the mother tongue, and even his proper Czech name Václav was forsaken among the French. He returned as a foreigner known as Karel. He encountered a deserted and impoverished land, prompting him to travel through Bohemia, offering aid in every way he could.

Karel assumed the Czech throne at the age of thirty (in 1346), possessing the wisdom of an elder and a comprehensive understanding of Europe. He was fluent in five languages, a cautious leader, and a wise ruler, acclaimed as the most educated monarch of his time. Having witnessed during his father's reign that wars brought no benefit to the land, he became a resolute advocate for peace.

His objective was to foster prosperity in Bohemia through peaceful means. With a paternalistic approach, he ensured the land was well cultivated, commerce thrived, and the sciences and arts flourished. Whenever conflicts arose within the German Empire, where the emperor was traditionally expected to mediate, he worked towards amicable resolutions, wielding gold as his weapon rather than a sword, allowing him to achieve his goals more expediently. He acquired land not through warfare, but through peaceful agreements and financial transactions.

Moreover, Karel was a deeply devout individual. The reconstructed St. Vitus Cathedral, the Church and Monastery of Emmaus, and the Charles Bridge in Prague, alongside numerous other churches and monasteries he founded and constructed, stand as testament to his piety. At Karlštejn, his beloved residence, there exists a narrow chamber where he would spend Easter week. In 1344, he successfully obtained from Pope Clement VI the elevation of the Prague Bishopric to an archbishopric, with the esteemed Arnošt of Pardubice appointed as its first archbishop. Karel extended an invitation to South Slavic monks to the Emmaus Monastery, where they conducted divine services in the Old Church Slavonic language, emulating the revered saints Cyril and Methodius. To this day, the Czech people refer to that church and monastery as 'na Slovanech' ('among the Slavs').

Karel not only inspired his nation with words to improve their country but also set a remarkable example himself. It is truly delightful to witness his diligent efforts in acquiring various elements from all corners of the world to enrich his land: he cultivated Czech wine using Burgundian grapes, invited renowned masters of art from near and far to grace Prague with their talents, adorned his residence and the capital city of Bohemia with magnificent edifices, and established prestigious universities, ensuring that the Czech people need not seek education abroad.

In 1348, with the invaluable assistance of Arnošt of Pardubice, Karel established the renowned University of Prague. He explicitly emphasized that it was his heartfelt priority and utmost concern that the Kingdom of Bohemia, which he cherished above all his other acquired lands, should not have to rely on foreign generosity due to its inherent wealth and abundance of intellectual treasures. With a multitude of wise men adorning the kingdom, he ensured that Bohemia would flourish and not constantly seek external assistance to quench its thirst for intellectual and artistic achievements.

In honor of this grand gesture, the University of Prague unveiled a magnificent monument during its 500th anniversary celebration in 1848 near the Charles Bridge (see the frontispiece image). At that time, prestigious universities were mainly found in southern and western European countries like Italy, Spain, France, and England. The establishment of this renowned educational institution in Prague brought great distinction to the city, and the Czechs took immense pride in their exceptional schools. Students and scholars of all ages, both locals and foreigners, flocked to the university in such numbers that housing became scarce. To address this, Karel founded the New Town of Prague, which still stands today, providing comfortable accommodation for the students.

Karel's expansion of the Czech Empire was achieved not through bloody wars but through peaceful agreements, combining inheritance and strategic purchases. He first acquired the Upper Palatinate, a region in present-day Bavaria beyond the Český Les, followed by Upper Lusatia. In 1364, he obtained the remaining parts of Silesia that his father Jan had not yet conquered, including the Duchies of Świdnica and Jawor, as well as Lower Lusatia. Finally, in 1373, he secured the Margraviate of Brandenburg.

Tragically, Karel passed away at the age of thirty-eight on November 29, 1378, in Prague. His reign had been characterized by peace, prosperity, and cultural advancement. He left a profound and enduring legacy as a wise and benevolent ruler, a patron of the arts and sciences, and a unifying figure for the Czech people. His extraordinary achievements earned him the esteemed title of "Father of the Homeland," and his reign is fondly remembered as a golden age in Czech history.

The St. Wenceslas Crown

The St. Wenceslas Crown holds a significant place in Czech history. It was crafted during the time of Charles from the purest Arabian gold, exemplifying exquisite craftsmanship. Atop the wreath that encircles the head, four large lilies proudly stand. These lilies are accompanied by two golden arches, forming a cross, with a small cross embedded within, adorned with thorns from the crown of Christ. Every element of the crown is embellished with precious pearls and uncut stones, including sapphires, emeralds, and rubies. The resplendence of this royal jewel surpasses all others, radiating the grandeur befitting of royal dignity. It is the enduring symbol of Czech monarchy, gracing the heads of Czech kings during their coronations.

Emperor Charles made a decree that the St. Wenceslas Crown must always be safeguarded within the main cathedral at St. Vitus on Prague Castle. Specifically, it should remain atop the head of St. Wenceslas at his tomb, untouched, except on the occasions of a Czech king's coronation or other significant events when it is to be displayed alongside the crown. Its primary purpose was to adorn the head of St. Wenceslas, hence its name - the St. Wenceslas Crown. This revered treasure serves as a timeless emblem of Czech history and sovereignty.

* * *

Charles was not only a wise ruler but also a loving family man. He dedicated himself to the upbringing of his sons: Wenceslas, Sigismund, and John. He cherished his Czech heritage, being proud of his descent from the renowned Přemyslid dynasty through his mother's side. In his efforts to promote equality, Charles ensured that the Czech population regained language rights equal to that of the Germans, decreeing the free use of the Czech language in city halls. The Germans also actively embraced the Czech language and diligently taught it to their children.

While valuing the well-being of his people, Charles was equally committed to maintaining law and order. During his stay in Italy, a wave of robberies plagued Bohemia, with Jan of Švihov, known as Pancíř, emerging as the main offender. Pancíř, who had previously been knighted by Charles himself and bestowed with a golden chain for his bravery, held the castle of Žampach. Upon his return, the emperor took personal action against this marauding knight, capturing him and his entire band. Pancíř, acknowledging his guilt, placed a hemp rope around his own neck, acknowledging that golden chains were not always deserved. Charles ordered the knight and his band to be hanged, ensuring justice prevailed.

Recognizing the need for improvements, Charles rectified flawed laws and introduced new, more sensible ones to better serve his subjects. Throughout his life, he had been married four times. His final wife, Elizabeth, a granddaughter of the Polish king, possessed extraordinary strength, able to twist silver plates into discs and break the strongest horseshoes with ease. In 1378, at the age of 63, the noble King Charles passed away. His body was laid to rest with great honor in the St. Vitus Cathedral, where it remains to this day. The Czech people hold his memory dear, bestowing upon him the title of "father of the homeland," a testament to his well-deserved legacy.

The Legend of Karlovy Vary

Once upon a time, the story goes, Karel arrived at Loket Castle. Eager for adventure, he embarked on a hunting expedition with a group of huntsmen and gentlemen, venturing into the dense forests that surrounded the area. As they pursued their prey, a magnificent stag, the chase led them across great distances. Eventually, the desperate stag made a daring leap onto the highest rock, seeking refuge and a chance to evade its pursuers. In a final act of desperation, the stag leaped into an immense abyss, hoping to secure its freedom. The hunting dog, unwavering in its loyalty, followed suit, but its howls of pain echoed through the valley as it encountered scalding hot water.

The hunters, alarmed by the dog's distress, traced its cries and circled the rock. As they descended into the valley, they witnessed the astonishing sight of water gushing from the rock. Recognizing the extraordinary nature of this phenomenon, Karel, with his keen insight, immediately summoned his physician from Loket Castle. The physician, after careful examination, declared the water to possess medicinal properties. Advising Karel to apply the water to his own leg wound, the physician's counsel proved successful as Karel experienced a swift recovery. Filled with gratitude for this divine blessing and the potential benefits it held, Karel established a hunting lodge and a house for the sick in that very location. He also extended an invitation for anyone who desired to settle there and build houses.

Since that fateful encounter, the city of Karlovy Vary[9] has emerged as a renowned and remarkable destination. People from all corners of Europe, and even from around the world, flock to this city seeking healing and rejuvenation. They partake in the restorative waters, either by drinking it or immersing themselves in therapeutic baths. The legacy of that extraordinary hunt lives on, as Karlovy Vary continues to attract thousands of

---

[9] This story holds the status of a legend, for the Eailovarshá springs were well-known to the Czech people long before Karel's time. In fact, the settlement in close proximity to these springs had already been referred to as Vary. The rivers that meander through the region where Vary is situated bear the names Teplá and Ohře, stemming from the concepts of warmth and heating. Nevertheless, it is indeed factual that Karel played a significant role in establishing a town near these springs in the year 1370, bestowing upon it the name "Karlovy Vary."

individuals in search of the restorative powers of its waters.

Arnošt of Pardubice

Good rulers are often surrounded by wise advisors and trusted friends. This was certainly the case with Karel, who found a steadfast companion in Arnošt of Pardubice, the first Archbishop of Prague.

Arnošt's birthplace is believed to be the castle known as "Hostinné," located in the present-day town of Hostinné nad Labem. His educational journey took him to various places, including a parish school in Kladsko, where his father served as a royal burgrave, as well as studies in Broumov, Prague, and Italy. Following his ordination as a priest, Arnošt served at St. Vitus Cathedral before ascending to the positions of bishop and, ultimately, archbishop.

With the establishment of the Archdiocese of Prague, Bohemia gained autonomy from the Archdiocese of Mainz, to which it had previously belonged. This pivotal period coincided with the presence of an exceptional and highly talented man as the archbishop - Arnošt. He wasted no time in implementing numerous regulations, adopting a stringent stance against unworthy clergy, and working tirelessly to ensure order and morality within the church. Additionally, he collaborated with the renowned archbishop to enact new laws, as well as amend or repeal outdated ones.

Arnošt was particularly vocal in advocating for the abolition of archaic practices known as "divine judgments" or "ordalia." These remnants of ancient pagan customs involved determining guilt or innocence through trials such as holding a hot iron or undergoing a test with boiling water when conclusive evidence was lacking. For instance, someone accused of theft would have to place their fingers on a hot iron to prove their innocence and swear an oath; if they were burned, they were considered guilty. Similarly, in property disputes, both the plaintiff and the defendant had to walk through deep water, with the one who perished being deemed the loser. Eventually, such matters were resolved through chance rather than these traditional methods.

Arnošt often accompanied Karel on his journeys and acted as his representative when visiting the pope, establishing a strong bond of love and trust between them. On several occasions, in Karel's absence, Arnošt assumed the role of regent, governing the country with diligence and care. His reputation as the first archbishop grew so significantly that even popes offered him higher positions of authority. Following the death of Pope Innocent VI, many cardinals considered electing Arnošt as the next pope. However, due to the customary practice of selecting only native Italians as pontiffs, this possibility did not come to fruition.

Arnošt possessed a deep appreciation for the arts and dedicated substantial resources to the construction of St. Vitus Cathedral. He also recognized the importance of education and played a pivotal role in the establishment of the University of Prague. He generously supported diligent students who displayed a genuine thirst for knowledge, ensuring they received the necessary resources for a comprehensive education.

Beyond his significant contributions to the public sphere, Arnošt distinguished himself through his exemplary private life. He led a devout, humble, and compassionate existence, extending kindness to all those he encountered. His charitable nature shone through during the severe famine that afflicted Bohemia in 1362. Arnošt's philanthropy provided crucial aid to those in need during this challenging time.

In 1364, this remarkable man passed away at his castle in Roudnice. True to his wishes, he was laid to rest in the main church in Kladsko, where it is said that he had even prepared his own tombstone during his lifetime. Arnošt's legacy endures as a testament to his unwavering devotion, profound humility, and commitment to the well-being of others.

Tomáš of Štítné

They say that good children are a precious treasure to their parents, and such was the case with Tomáš of Štítné. His parents named him after their ancestral fortress, Štítné, which now stands as a small village near Počátky on the Moravian border. Tomáš was deeply cherished by his parents, who instilled in him a strong devotion to prayer, a diligent attendance of church services, a joyful contemplation of God, and a compassionate nature towards others. Following in the footsteps of his parents, Tomáš excelled in his faith, never straying from his love for God. However, tragedy struck when his beloved parents passed away, leaving Tomáš as a poor orphan. Inheriting the Štítné fortress and all its possessions brought him no joy in his state of loneliness. Seeking further knowledge that couldn't be obtained at home, he set off for Prague to attend the newly established university, embarking on this journey at the age of approximately 23.

Having gained a wealth of knowledge during his time in Prague, Tomáš eventually returned to his tranquil fortress. There, he led a peaceful and devout life, seeking solace in his faith. God blessed him with children whom he loved dearly, just as his own parents had loved him. I can envision him sitting among his children, imparting his teachings on the Christian faith. In order to help them retain these invaluable lessons, he meticulously documented his teachings in a book called "ŘeČi besední" (Discourses).

Later, Tomáš of Štítné took his teachings and divided them into smaller sections or books, known as "O obecních věcech křesťanských" (On General Christian Matters). How eagerly his children devoured these books, bringing joy to their father's heart. He had devoted himself to his children, nurturing them in the holy faith and shielding them from the misleading teachings of the world. Yet, diligent Tomáš did not neglect his fellow countrymen. He penned a profoundly instructive book specifically for them, pouring out his heart, soul, experience, and teachings. This book, titled "Ěeči sváteční" (Festive Discourses), delved into Christian matters based on the holy Gospel.

However, God put Tomáš to the test in various ways. His son Jan fell under the influence of wicked companions, refusing to heed his father's wise advice. The poor old man suffered greatly due to his ungrateful child, experiencing the deep pain of a child's ingratitude. And what awaited such a disobedient child after death? Only punishment and rigorous penance. This burdened the venerable old man even more. He found solace in his devoted daughter Aneska, who cherished reading his books. But when she passed away, the kind old man was left without someone to share his troubles and find comfort in. He revised his teachings once more, knowing that his time on Earth was coming to an end. And soon after, he peacefully passed away.

With Tomáš's departure, it seemed as if the angel of peace had deserted the Czech homeland for a prolonged period. Unforeseen wars and disputes emerged, casting a shadow over the land. The absence of Štítné, the symbol of tranquility, was deeply felt, leaving a void that would be felt for years to come.

Václav IV

Anticipating his imminent passing, Charles IV made a significant decision in 1377, dividing his lands among his three sons. Vácslav was granted Bohemia, Silesia, and a portion of Lusatia, Sigmund received Brandenburg, and Jan inherited the remaining part of Lusatia. Moravia, on the other hand, was bestowed upon Jošt, the eldest son of Jan and Charles' brother. While this division of power occurred, it unfortunately resulted in a significant weakening of the Czech kingdom, which was already in a fragile state.

Václav, also known as the fourth of his name, was an educated, worthy, and fair ruler. However, he struggled with indulging in his passions, often lacking control over them. His stubbornness and inflexibility became a hindrance, as his fiery temper and occasional lack of mental acuity impacted his decision-making. He possessed a strong affinity for pastimes, particularly hunting, which consumed a significant amount of his time that could have been better allocated to the welfare of his subjects. Nonetheless, Václav did exhibit prudence when it came to financial matters, refraining from imposing heavy taxes on the people. He frequently mingled with the common folk, at times even disguising himself to ensure the proper observance of order and justice. The "common people" held a deep affection for him. Under his reign, complete security prevailed in Bohemia, to the extent that it was said a child wearing a golden crown on its head could safely travel throughout the land. To gain a deeper understanding of the working class's conditions, Václav dedicated an entire day to working in a vineyard alongside laborers. He used this experience to enact laws regulating work hours and rest periods.

Václav also displayed a willingness to appoint individuals of lower status to various positions whenever possible, which, unsurprisingly, drew the ire of many nobles. However, he proved capable of suppressing their discontent through the use of military force.

During this period, Germany was engulfed in turmoil. A schism within the church had given rise to two popes, causing discord among secular rulers and disobedience among the lower clergy. In Bohemia, a dispute erupted between King Václav and Archbishop Jan of Jenštejn, who consistently opposed the king's actions whenever possible. Unfortunately, a regrettable incident occurred that further fueled tensions: King Václav planned to convert Kladruby Abbey into a bishopric and had instructed his officials to inform him immediately upon the abbot's passing, so that a new abbot would not be elected. However, when news of the abbot's death took an unusually long time to reach the king, he inquired about the abbot's wellbeing.

To his surprise, he was informed that the abbot had indeed passed away, but the archbishop's vicar, Jan of Pomuk, had already confirmed the appointment of a new abbot. This greatly angered the king, leading to his resentment towards the archbishop and his officials. The archbishop hastily fled to Koudnice, while some members of the chapter were temporarily arrested, although later released. Tragically, two individuals, including the vicar Jan of Pomuk, endured torture and were subsequently thrown off a bridge into the Vltava River. The king deeply regretted this act, but his attempts to reconcile with the archbishop were met with deceit. As a consequence, even the Prague chapter sided with the king, while the archbishop chose to seek refuge in Rome.

Furthermore, certain Czech lords grew resentful of Václav's detachment from governance, leading them to plot against him. While staying at Králové Dvůr near Beroun during the summer in his Žebrák Castle, the king was captured by these conspiring lords and imprisoned first in Prague and later in Austria. Under duress, he was compelled to appoint Jošt, the Margrave of Moravia, as the highest steward of the kingdom. However, Václav managed to secretly communicate his dire situation to his brother Jan, who made proclamations from Hor Kutná, rallying the nation to his cause. People flocked to Jan's side, and even German princes dispatched troops to secure the king's liberation, resulting in Václav's eventual release.

From that moment onward, the king grew increasingly distrustful and found solace in drinking. His brother Sigmund, who had ascended to the throne of Hungary, also proved insincere towards Václav and harbored ambitions for power in Bohemia. Sigmund imprisoned Václav in Vienna, but the resilient king swiftly liberated himself, prompting Sigmund's hasty retreat to Hungary after ruling for only a brief period.

It is worth noting that Václav held the title of King of Germany as well, although he paid little attention to German affairs due to their dire state at the time.

Master Jan Hus

The town of Husinec is situated above the Planice River in Písek. In the era of Charles, there resided a humble farmer with a son named Jan. Jan possessed exceptional academic abilities and ardently implored his father to send him to Prague for higher education. Unfortunately, due to financial constraints, his father couldn't fulfill his wish. However, fortune smiled upon Jan when a prosperous nobleman named Mikuláš from Husinec learned of his plight. Recognizing Jan's potential, Mikuláš took him under his patronage and sponsored his studies in Prague.

Jan thrived in his educational pursuits, eventually becoming a priest and a distinguished theology teacher at the universities in Prague. His exceptional abilities led to him serving as the rector or director of those esteemed institutions. Later, he became a renowned preacher at the Bethlehem Chapel, captivating audiences with his sermons. In addition to his theological acumen, Jan also held mastery over liberal arts, which today would equate to a doctorate in philosophy.

Through his charismatic preaching, Jan garnered immense respect and admiration, with even Queen Žofie, the wife of King Václav, entrusting him as her confessor. His esteemed reputation extended to the nobility, who held him in high regard. It was during this time that a young nobleman named Jerome of Prague, fresh from completing his studies at the University of Oxford in England, approached Jan. Jerome shared with Jan the writings of John Wycliffe, which expounded upon various aspects of Christian doctrine. Jan was deeply captivated by Wycliffe's teachings, leading him to incorporate and publicly preach about them at the university.

Meanwhile, King Václav found himself embroiled in a dispute with Pope Gregory XII of Rome and aligned himself with Pope Benedict of Avignon. The Czech masters, including Hus and Jerome, along with the students, rallied behind the king. However, the Archbishop and the chapter remained loyal to the Roman Pope, and amidst the ensuing chaos, the church council in Pisa elected a new pope, Alexander V, while declaring Gregory and Benedict deposed. This only intensified the prevailing turmoil of the time.

While Hus was still in Prague, significant disputes erupted between the Czech and German factions at the University of Prague. The university had a larger population of German students, as Charles IV had granted them numerous privileges and incentives to attract them to study there. In that period, Prague boasted thousands of students, encompassing various age groups. During voting, foreign students were granted three votes, while Czech students only had one. Consequently, the Germans consistently secured the best and most lucrative positions, perpetuating injustice by sidelining deserving Czech individuals. Hus, a passionate patriot and champion of Czech rights, vehemently opposed this inequity. He brought the matter to the attention of King Václav, who harbored frustrations with the Germans for causing him numerous troubles. Václav decided that henceforth, the domestic nation (including the German residents of our land) would possess three votes, while all foreigners would have a single collective vote. This decision enraged a significant portion of the German student body and faculty, leading them to leave Prague in anger and establish their own universities in Leipzig. However, they soon regretted their hasty choice when they reminisced about the vibrant academic atmosphere of Prague.

Once Hus had rid himself of his adversaries through this resolution, he resumed his preaching activities. He asserted that Wycliffe's teachings were not as dire as commonly believed, but rather were being misinterpreted. Nonetheless, the archbishop took action and condemned Wycliffe's books, publicly ordering their burning and forbidding Hus from delivering sermons. However,

Hus did not comply and continued preaching with even greater fervor. It is worth noting that Hus did deviate in certain aspects of his teachings, particularly regarding his doctrine on predestination and the notion of individuals being destined for eternal blessedness or damnation.

During that period, Pope John XXIII, who was deemed unworthy, initiated a conflict against Ladislaus, the King of Naples. The pope dispatched priests across Christian lands to preach indulgences and collect contributions for this war effort. Hus adamantly preached against this practice, leading to further disputes and divisions, as some aligned with the papal decrees while others rallied behind Hus. The king chose to remain silent, carefully observing the unfolding situation. Another significant event took place when the city council executed three young men who had refused to comply with the indulgence preachers. This act stirred public outrage, with the people proclaiming the executed individuals as martyrs. Hus, with great solemnity, buried them in Bethlehem Chapel. Subsequently, a curse was placed upon Hus, resulting in the prohibition of divine services and all religious ceremonies in Prague as long as he remained within the city limits. This ecclesiastical punishment, known as an interdict, was imposed. In response, Hus left Prague and took his message of God's word and teachings to the rural areas, while also devoting time to writing. Hus possessed exceptional writing skills and was a truly erudite individual. We owe him particular gratitude for his contributions to the advancement of Czech orthography.

Through the efforts of Emperor Sigismund, a new church council was convened in Constance, situated on the southern shore of Lake Constance. The council aimed to address the unity of Church leadership, church reforms, and the suppression of Hus' and Wycliffe's teachings. Sigismund provided Hus with a safe-conduct letter, guaranteeing his safety during the journey and return. Relying on this assurance, Hus embarked on his journey to Constance without fear. However, the emperor did not honor his commitment. The council deemed Hus a heretic, leading to his subsequent condemnation and execution by burning at the stake on July 6, 1415.

Approximately a year later, Jerome, a friend of Hus from Prague, met a similar fate and was also burned at the stake.

Eneas Sylvius, who would later become a pope, penned the following words about both men: "Both faced death with unwavering courage, proceeding to the stake as if attending a feast, exhibiting no signs of sorrow. As the flames engulfed them, they sang hymns, only momentarily interrupted by the crackling of the fire. No wise individual has displayed as much fortitude in the face of death as these men upon the stake."

Jan Žižka of Trocnov

The burning of Hus by Emperor Sigismund sparked deep anger among the Czechs, who viewed it as a profound humiliation to their entire nation. In response, they embraced Hus's teachings even more passionately, adopting the name Hussites and incorporating both forms of communion, partaking of both bread and wine.

Leading the Hussites was the renowned Jan Žižka of Trocnov, who had lost one eye. He organized his forces into a dynamic stronghold known as the "Wagenburg." The Wagenburg comprised the following components:

A) Outer row of wagons.
R) Middle row of wagons.
C) Enclosed wings.
D) Open space.

a) Groups of soldiers, including axemen, spearmen, and archers, positioned strategically around the wagons, defending them.

b) Mounted soldiers with horses ready to dismount from the wagons.

c) Cannons placed in front of the gates between the wagons, operated by a skilled crew.

d) Additional reserve forces available for reinforcement.

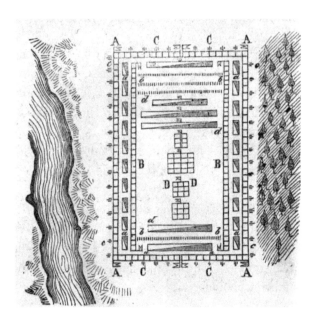

Jan Žižka of Trocnov, a courageous Czech knight, led the Hussites during these tumultuous times. His skills in warfare were renowned, and even King Václav held him in high regard, appointing him as his chamberlain. The Hussites, under Žižka's command, organized grand processions in Prague, but their peaceful march was disrupted when someone from the New Town Hall hurled a stone at their priest. Enraged by this act, the Hussites stormed into the hall and forcefully ejected thirteen councilors, most of whom were Germans. Those below the windows engaged in combat, wielding spears and flails against the councilors.

Upon hearing of the incident, King Václav suffered a stroke and tragically passed away in 1419, plunging the Czechs into mourning. This marked the beginning of a period of disorder and the eruption of the Hussite war, which brought immense devastation to our beloved homeland. Those were dark days indeed. The majority of the Czech nation stood firmly with Hus and his allies, while their adversaries consisted primarily of Germans and certain nobles.

Following Václav's death, the Hussites targeted the monasteries, expelling monks who refused to administer communion under both forms. The situation escalated when the German miners from Kutná Hora added fuel to the fire. They purchased captured Hussites and callously cast them alive into mine shafts. These gruesome acts only intensified the animosity between the two factions.

But the Czechs showed no fear. They rallied behind the courageous leadership of Jan Žižka, a truly remarkable figure. Žižka seized control of Lesser Town and cornered the widowed Queen Žofie in the Royal Castle, compelling her to seek peace. Meanwhile, Emperor Sigismund arrived in Bohemia with a formidable army and shamelessly ravaged the land. He set up camp just outside Prague, but the Czechs, led by Žižka, scoffed at him. They launched a fierce assault, decisively defeating Sigismund and forcing him to flee from Bohemia. When Žižka subdued the Vyšehrad garrison, who remained loyal to Sigismund, the emperor returned a second time, seeking revenge and support for his cause. Yet, he faced defeat once more. Žižka vanquished him beneath Vyšehrad, expelled him from the land, and laid waste to the fortress. With Prague firmly under Hussite control, Žižka and his forces embarked on a campaign into the countryside. They conquered towns aligned with Sigismund and dealt with those who refused to join their cause. The emperor and his allies were powerless. Despite their numerous attempts to subdue Žižka, they achieved nothing. Fear of Žižka and the Hussites gripped all who heard their name, and none dared to confront them. At the mere mention of "The Hussites are coming!" panic would seize the enemy forces, causing them to flee in terror.

During the siege of Rábí Castle, Žižka suffered the loss of his second eye, rendering him blind. Yet, he refused to yield to anyone and continued as the unwavering leader of the Hussites. He captured numerous towns and villages, laid waste to countless castles, and emerged victorious in multiple battles. The fear he instilled was so great that no one dared to challenge him anymore, for no one could defeat him.

Despite his blindness, Žižka devised a strategic arrangement of his war wagons, ensuring that the enemy could not approach from any direction. Any attempt to do so resulted in their swift retreat with heavy casualties. He stood as the most renowned warrior of his era, revolutionizing the art of warfare with his innovative tactics.

However, during the siege of Přibyslav, Žižka fell suddenly ill and tragically passed away in the open field on October 11, 1424. Before his death, he urged his brothers to remain steadfast in the truth of God and to maintain a deep reverence for Him.

Feast of the Hussite Cherries

Even in the aftermath of Žižka's death, the Taborites displayed unwavering bravery and resolve. Leading them was Prokop Holý, also known as Prokop the Great, a fearless priest and warrior. Under his guidance, the Czech forces achieved resounding victories over the Germans at Ostrý in 1426, and in subsequent years at Tachov and Domažlice in 1431. They had grown weary of the relentless German incursions into their land and sought retribution. As a result, they ventured into neighboring territories, engaging in plunder and looting across Austria, Moravia, Hungary, Silesia, Lusatia, Brandenburg, Saxony, Meissen, Bavaria, and other regions. Their approach instilled great fear, and people trembled at the mere mention of the approaching Hussites. Towns and villages were abandoned as residents fled to the safety of forests. The Czech forces showed no mercy, pillaging settlements before setting them ablaze. Revenge was their motivation.

For instance, prior to the Battle of Ostrý, when a massive German force of 70,000 invaded Bohemia, the Czechs sent a message to them, appealing for fair treatment of prisoners and assuring reciprocal kindness if victory favored them. However, the Germans, arrogant and confident in their triumph, scorned the Czechs, refusing to provide sustenance to the "heretics." This derogatory response compelled the Czechs to respond in kind.

During a single campaign, Prokop the Great pillaged over a hundred towns and castles, returning to Bohemia with immeasurable spoils. Their relentless pursuit of vengeance knew no bounds.

Once, Prokop led his Taborite forces to the outskirts of Naumburg, a Saxon town. Setting up camp on a nearby hill, he sought to send a strong message to the town's inhabitants. Two captured peasants were dispatched with a written ultimatum: surrender or face destruction by fire and sword without mercy. The people of Naumburg trembled with fear, but their resolve to resist remained strong. They penned a plea for mercy, urging Prokop to spare their town without requiring their surrender. Upon receiving their response, Prokop's anger flared, and he firmly declared that no mercy would be granted unless they surrendered immediately. Panic gripped the town as the residents anticipated their impending doom. Tearful farewells were exchanged, and lamentations filled the air.

However, amidst the despair, a locksmith named Vilém Wolf proposed a daring plan to save their beloved town. He advised the people of Naumburg to dress their children in white garments the following day and send them, accompanied by armed citizens, to the enemy camp. The children would kneel before Prokop, beseeching him for mercy with tears streaming down their faces. The townspeople embraced this idea wholeheartedly.

At the appointed hour, 238 boys and 221 girls gathered in front of the town hall. Escorted by two hundred armed citizens, they made their way towards the camp. As Prokop beheld this unexpected procession from his tent, he was struck with astonishment. It appeared to him as if a choir of angels had descended, pleading for mercy. Moved by their innocent plea, the victorious leader's heart softened. He bent down and kissed the pale cheeks of the children. Prokop then called for musicians, who entertained the children as they were treated to wine, cherries, pears, and peas. The atmosphere transformed from fear to joy as the relieved children joyfully danced around their Taborite savior. As twilight approached, Prokop addressed the children, urging them to hurry back to their anxious parents. At the gate, they were instructed to shout, "Victory of the Hussites!" and deliver the news of mercy bestowed upon their city. Prokop assured them that the Czech army would depart the next day without harm to the town or its residents. This extraordinary event occurred on July 28, 1432.

To commemorate this miraculous occasion, the people of Naumburg gather each year at the very field where the Hussite camp stood. They indulge in fruits and wine, celebrating the enduring spirit of their ancestors. Following the festivities, they venture to the pea fields, where they joyfully pluck peas without restraint. This annual celebration has become known as the "Feast of the Hussite Cherries," a testament to the mercy and hope that once triumphed over fear and despair.

Battle of Lipany

Soon enough, Sigismund came to the realization that the Hussites couldn't be defeated through sheer force. He opted for a different approach: seeking reconciliation with them. Emperor Sigismund and Pope Eugene IV issued orders for the gathering of princes and bishops in Basel, Switzerland, in 1432. The purpose was to address the religious and general disorder that plagued the region. The Czech delegation also made their way to Basel, with notable figures like Jan Rokycana, the pastor of Týn Church, and Prokop Holý, accompanied by three hundred skilled knights. The news of the Czechs' arrival caused a stir in Basel, and its inhabitants poured out in large numbers to catch a glimpse of the renowned Czech warriors, whose exploits had made Europe tremble. Excited voices pointed to Prokop the Great, acknowledging him as the indomitable leader of the valiant Taborites, who had achieved countless victories. Negotiations commenced both in Basel and Prague, resulting in the granting of some of the Hussites' demands outlined in their articles. The Pope himself signed the treaty, welcoming the Czechs back into the fold of the Catholic Church.

However, the Taborites and the Orphans, unsatisfied with the treaty, continued their struggle against the Catholics and the citizens of Prague. The Prague citizens allied themselves with the royal forces, led by Diviš Bořek of Miletín, in opposition to the Taborites. Yet, the Taborites joined forces once again with the Orphans, resolutely facing their adversaries. The Czech armies, akin to two dark clouds, advanced towards each other, ready to determine an outcome that Europe had been unable to impose on them. The decisive battle unfolded on May 30, 1434, at Lipany, between Kouřim and Český Brod. Employing their trademark war wagons, the Taborites engaged in combat. Aware of the Taborites' invincibility in this strategy, Bořek feigned retreat, prompting the Taborites to abandon their wagons and pursue him. Suddenly, Bořek turned with great force to launch a counter-attack against the Taborites. A ferocious struggle ensued as Czechs fiercely fought one another. However, the Taborites failed to regroup. When their cavalry leaders fled, surrender became inevitable. Prokop the Great seethed with rage, his face marked by despair. The victorious star of the Taborites had finally waned. Even Prokop the Little, the leader of the Orphans, and other prominent Taborite commanders perished in the battle. It was an overwhelming defeat for the

Taborites, with most of them either slain or captured. Only a small group of approximately 300 infantrymen managed to escape, and they valiantly resisted the royal forces for two more years.

And so, the Czechs suffered defeat at the hands of their fellow countrymen, marking the temporary end of the Hussite war that had ravaged Central Europe for fifteen long years. The state of our beloved homeland during that period was truly disheartening. The once magnificent Kingdom of Charles had been transformed beyond recognition. Desolation and pillaged lands stretched before the eyes of travelers, seemingly pleading for mercy. Neglected cities and impoverished villages stood as pitiful remnants of the tumultuous past. Instead of towering castles, ruins now pierced the sky. The toil and achievements of countless centuries lay in ruins. Our homeland had never experienced such profound misfortune as it did throughout the Hussite conflicts. It was during this time that Sigismund, the deceitful brother of Wenceslas, ascended to the throne as the King of Bohemia. However, his reign was short-lived, as he passed away in Znojmo just two years later. With no direct heirs, his son-in-law, Albert of Austria, assumed the throne as the new king.

King Ladislav and Jan Jiskra

In 1439, Emperor Albert II passed away, and it was only after his death that his son, Ladislav, was born. Queen Elizabeth, Ladislav's mother, appointed Emperor Frederick IV as the regent for her son, who also happened to be Ladislav's uncle. Many valiantly defended Ladislav's rights, with one individual standing out among them: Jan Jiskra.

Jan Jiskra of Brandýs hailed from a noble family in Moravia. Drawn to the life of a soldier, he relinquished his ancestral lands at a young age and ventured abroad to train in the art of warfare. Upon his return to Bohemia, he assumed leadership of the Táborites, whom Emperor Sigismund dispatched to confront the Turks. Jiskra engaged in three fierce battles against the Turks, fought between the Danube and the Sava rivers. In the final clash, the Turks suffered a brutal defeat. Gripped by terror, they plunged into the Sava one after another, along with their horses, meeting a watery demise. Others were enticed and driven into the treacherous mud and marshes, where they met a miserable end.

Jiskra's reputation spread far and wide, leading Queen Elizabeth to appoint him as the highest captain of King Ladislav. With his forces, he swiftly seized control of the entire region of Slovakia and engaged in numerous intense battles against the adversaries of the king. Fortune smiled upon Jiskra in these encounters, as he repeatedly vanquished and dispersed forces numbering 6,000 to 8,000 with his own contingent of 5,000 to 6,000 soldiers.

Once, Jiskra made a visit to Nové Město near Vienna to meet the six-year-old king, whom he had been fighting for without even knowing him. When he laid eyes upon the child's beauty and the earnestness in his gaze, tears of joy welled up in his eyes, and he knelt down to kiss the young king's hand. Overwhelmed with emotion, he spoke, "At last, I see you, my king! If only you knew the trials and tribulations I have endured for your sake! Look at my scars! I have dedicated my life to your father and to you! Though you may not yet grasp it, may God grant me the time when you will recognize those who have been loyal to you. I will always be by your side!" Jiskra then presented the royal orphan with some gifts and inquired, "What will you give me in return for my service? What reward will you grant your highest captain?"

Coincidentally, the king's almoner was present and said to the young prince, "This is your highest captain, O noble king. Will you bestow a reward upon him?" Upon hearing these words, the young prince glanced around for a moment and, not having his own bowl, reached for the almoner's bowl. He took out six copper coins that were inside and handed them to Jiskra. Jiskra had these coins transformed into gold and always wore them around his neck, remarking that this gift signified the generosity and kind-heartedness that King Ladislav would possess. And indeed, his premonition came true. Ladislav, who ascended to the throne in 1452, proved to be a good, generous, and beloved ruler. However, in 1457, just as he anticipated the arrival of his bride, Magdalena of France, he passed away unexpectedly in Prague. This left two powerful kingdoms, the Kingdom of Bohemia and the Kingdom of Hungary, orphaned and in mourning.

George of Poděbrady

George of Poděbrady stands as one of the most eminent rulers of the 15th century. Hailing from a noble family in Moravia, he possessed a multi-faceted character. Not particularly tall, he had fair skin and a genial countenance. His noble and just conduct garnered him immense respect among his fellow countrymen, leading to his election as the king of Bohemia following the demise of Ladislaus in 1458.

George governed Bohemia with sagacity, devoting his utmost attention to rectifying the damage inflicted by previous tumultuous times. His endeavors aimed to restore the golden era of Charles IV within the region. He undertook measures to improve the currency, fostered industry and trade, and shielded his subjects from the pressures exerted by the influential elite. He displayed kindness towards the common people, demanded accountability from the nobles, and ensured justice for all. Consequently, the ancient monastic orders returned to the land, ushering in an era of peace, serenity, and the revival of various crafts and artistic endeavors. Prosperity accompanied their resurgence. Alas, this blessed era of tranquility was not destined to endure for long.

Pope Pius II, a highly erudite individual, observed the remarkable calm prevailing in Bohemia and implored King George to renounce the Articles or Compacts granted to the Czechs by the Council of Basel. However, the Czechs were unwilling to relinquish what had cost them significant effort and bloodshed. King George himself refused to comply, fearing the emergence of fresh storms within the land. As a consequence, the pope issued a curse against him in 1464, extending the same anathema to all those who remained loyal to him as their king. In response, his adversaries united, forming an alliance known as the Zelenohorská League, comprising individuals from Moravia, Silesia, Lusatia, and other regions.

Meanwhile, George contemplated the daunting task of repelling the Turks and reclaiming Europe from their grasp. Following their capture of Constantinople, the capital of the Greek Empire, in 1453, the Turks grew in power, posing an increasing threat to the entirety of Europe. They expanded their control over the Greek-Slavic peninsula and plundered Hungary, endangering all Christians. King George fervently urged the princes to unite against this common enemy. Recognized as one of the bravest Christian rulers, many desired to elect him as the deputy of the emperor and bestow upon him supreme leadership in the joint campaign against the Turks. However, George remained burdened by the lingering curse, which prevented him from assuming the role of the Roman Emperor or the highest commander of the anti-Turkish forces. Sadly, the pope succeeded in diverting the crusader army from fighting the Turks to invade Bohemia instead, wreaking havoc and devastation upon the land.

Amidst these trying circumstances, Matthias Corvinus, the King of Hungary, launched an attack against George. Seizing the opportunity, the pope offered him the Bohemian crown. Despite the adversity that befell him, George did not lose hope. The exceptional Czech army intercepted the crusaders near Nýrsko and achieved a resounding victory, scattering their forces and leaving only a handful to escape across the borders in 1467. Meanwhile, George and his courageous sons, Viktorin and Jindřich (or Hynek), valiantly opposed Matthias. They fiercely confronted him, compelling him to suffer significant losses and retreat to Austria. During his second attempt to invade Bohemia, George decisively defeated him at Vilémov, trapping Matthias and his entire army like prey in a trap. In desperation, Matthias had to beg for a truce in 1469. However, amidst these ongoing conflicts, George passed away in 1471. As he lay on his deathbed, he imparted his wisdom to the Czechs, advising them to select Vladislav, the son of the Polish king Casimir IV, as his successor to the Bohemian throne. In this way, this esteemed ruler quietly sowed the seeds of contentment, knowing that he had done everything within his power to benefit his beloved homeland.

King Vladislav II

King Vladislav II was known as a well-meaning but feeble ruler due to his tendency to respond with "dobře" (good) to everything. Consequently, he earned the nickname King Dobře. Following the death of Matthias in 1490, the Hungarian nobles also elected him as their king. From that point on, he resided in Buda, the capital of Hungary. King Vladislav had two children, Anna and Ludvík.

During this period, Maximilian I of the Habsburg dynasty held the title of King of Germany. Vladislav sought to establish a family connection with Maximilian and traveled with his children to Vienna to visit him. Maximilian eagerly welcomed them and went out of his way to meet them. After a few days, the two rulers agreed to arrange a marriage between their children. Ludvík, Vladislav's son, would marry Maria, an Austrian princess, once he reached adulthood. Furthermore, one of Maximilian's grandsons, either Karl or Ferdinand, would wed Anna, Vladislav's daughter. They also stipulated that if Ludvík had no offspring, Anna and her future husband would succeed him on the throne.

Satisfied with the arrangement, Vladislav returned to Hungary but passed away in 1516. As a result, ten-year-old Ludvík ascended to the thrones of Bohemia and Hungary. Until he reached adulthood, he was under the guardianship of Sigismund, the King of Poland, and Maximilian, the King of Germany. Ludvík proved to be a conscientious and diligent young man. He remained primarily in Hungary, only making a brief visit to his cherished Bohemia six years later. However, he couldn't stay long as the Turks posed a threat to Hungary. Sultan Suleiman gathered a formidable army of 200,000 warriors and sent a message to the Hungarians, demanding their voluntary surrender. He aimed to conquer Hungary and Germany, intending to dismantle the Christian empire.

Faced with the daunting message, the young king felt a sense of urgency and swiftly mobilized an army. However, how could he stand against an adversary ten times more powerful? They managed to gather a force of approximately 25,000 soldiers. Despite the overwhelming odds, Ludvík did not succumb to fear. Seasoned leaders from Bohemia and Poland advised him to wait for the arrival of experienced troops from Bohemia and Moravia before engaging in battle. However, certain proud Hungarian lords urged him to launch an immediate attack against the Turks. Not fully comprehending the intricacies of warfare, Ludvík heeded their voices and fearlessly charged at the enemy. Unfortunately, he was met with defeat and compelled to retreat. The battlefield became a grim sight, strewn with fallen Hungarian soldiers, many of whom were taken captive or left wounded. The king found himself in a desperate flight. Tragically, fate dealt a cruel blow as the young king and his horse became ensnared in the treacherous mud, meeting a tragic end.

The widowed queen, Maria, grieved the loss of her youthful husband. Determined to locate his body, she arranged a grand funeral procession. The remains of this ill-fated king now rest in the royal tomb at Buda Castle. Maria, consumed by sorrow, continued to mourn ceaselessly. Despite her appointment as regent in the Netherlands by her brother, she remained steadfast in her mourning attire.

And thus, the Czechs found themselves without a king once more. The Archduke Ferdinand of Austria was expected to assume the throne as the King of Bohemia. However, the Czechs rejected his claim, asserting their right to choose their own monarch in accordance with their own wishes. In response, the highest burgrave, Lev of Rožmitál, summoned a general assembly in Prague. Lords, knights, and envoys from the royal cities convened for this crucial gathering. They selected eight representatives from each estate who, bound by their solemn oath, would vote based on their conscience and judgment to determine the most deserving candidate. These twenty-four chosen delegates then gathered in the chapel of St. Wenceslas at Prague Castle to deliberate.

Outside the church, an eager crowd of thousands eagerly awaited the announcement of their chosen king. Finally, the doors swung open, and the highest burgrave addressed the people, declaring, "Ferdinand, the Archduke of Austria, is now the King of Bohemia!"

And thus, the Kingdom of Bohemia came under the governance of the Habsburg dynasty, which has remained the case until recent times[10].

---

[10] Please note that this information is based on a translation of historical events up until 1873, and subsequent developments have occurred since then.

Three Famous Czech Men

The noble Pernštejn family of Czech-Moravian descent was truly remarkable, but its most illustrious member was Vilém of Pernštejn, who stood among the foremost figures of his era. Widely respected and cherished, he earned a reputation for his boundless generosity, unwavering fairness, and tireless commitment to the common good. With exceptional managerial skills, he amassed substantial wealth, acquiring a multitude of estates and castles. His noble qualities were blessed by God.

As the highest governor in Bohemia, Vilém lamented the presence of Czech individuals driven by self-interest and greed, sowing discord to exploit others. He made earnest efforts to reconcile conflicts and foster unity and love. He once declared, "Even if I were half-dead, I would gladly do everything in my power to promote harmony." However, while seeking to resolve new disputes among Czech estates, this virtuous man passed away in 1521 in Pardubice. His memory will forever endure.

During the same period, Bohuslav of Lobkowicz from Hasistein resided in Bohemia. Despite his youth, he diligently pursued studies in Italy and Paris, and he embarked on extensive travels throughout Asia and Africa. Swiftly gaining renown, he emerged as the preeminent scholar of his time. Yet Bohuslav did not seek personal fame and glory; on the contrary, he remained remarkably modest and dedicated his life to the pursuit of knowledge and other noble endeavors.

Additionally, he displayed great talent as a poet. He endeavored to eradicate pernicious vices in the nation, such as extravagance and licentiousness. Bohuslav admonished the Czech estates and offered valuable counsel and warnings to King Vladislav. At that time, the Czech nobility took pride in having such an eminent figure among them, though it would have been preferable had they all followed his example. Nonetheless, many individuals sought to serve the country and its people in accordance with his teachings. The privileged class treated their subjects with kindness, and the affluent provided assistance to the less fortunate. In general, those who adhered to Bohuslav's words found themselves dedicated to serving God and the people.

Tragically, the esteemed Bohuslav met an untimely demise at a young age in 1509, at the tender age of 48. Another remarkable figure deserving of recognition is Viktorin Kornel of Všehrdy, the son of a neighboring town in Chrudim. He exhibited exceptional prowess in the liberal arts during his time at esteemed universities and went on to deliver lectures on wisdom. Later, he assumed the role of a notary for the land registry. In recognition of his contributions to science and the nation, King Vladislav II bestowed him with ennoblement. Viktorin's notable work, "Nine Books on the Laws and Judgments of the Bohemian Land Registry," stands as a testament to his deep love for his homeland and its legal system. While Bohuslav of Lobkowicz primarily composed works in Latin, Viktorin embraced the Czech language and labored diligently to advance its development. Sadly, he passed away in 1520.

During that same era, numerous Czech intellectuals were actively engaged in fostering national enlightenment. Among them were Čehoř Hrubý of Jelení, Ctibor Tovačovský of Cimburk, Václav of Písek, Mikuláš Konáč of Hodišíkov, and many others who played significant roles in this endeavor.

Daniel Adam of Veleslavín

During the reign of King Ferdinand I, there lived a wise miller named Štěpán Adam in Veleslavín near Prague. He took great pride in his son, Daniel, who displayed remarkable abilities that brought him immense joy. Upon reaching adulthood, Daniel embarked on a teaching career at the University of Prague in 1568, at the young age of twenty-two.

Coincidentally, Prokop Lupáč, who taught history at the university, decided to step down from his position. Given Daniel's extensive knowledge and deep engagement with history since his youth, he was widely recognized as the foremost expert in Bohemia. The Czech people eagerly requested that he assume the role vacated by Lupáč, an invitation that Adam gladly accepted. For seven years, he taught history with utmost dedication and garnered immense praise. His lecture hall brimmed with eager students, attentively absorbing the words of their beloved instructor.

In due course, Adam married Anna, the eldest daughter of the esteemed printer Jiří Melantrich of

Aventin. Reluctantly, he decided to resign from his teaching post, leaving his students disheartened. However, owing to his remarkable accomplishments, he received a noble title and henceforth was known as Dan Adam of Veleslavín. Tragically, shortly after, his father-in-law passed away, and Daniel Adam transitioned into the field of printing.

Don't imagine that books have always been printed. In ancient times, books were painstakingly copied by hand, requiring extensive labor and expense. The Holy Scriptures alone were valued at several hundred gold coins. This meant that knowledge and the arts were limited to the privileged few, while the less fortunate struggled to access them. It wasn't until the mid-15th century that Johannes Gutenberg and J. Faust in Mainz achieved the breakthrough of carving letters and printing books. The art of printing eventually reached Bohemia, much to the delight of all. Now, people could obtain essential books at an affordable price and delve into knowledge across various fields.

The first printing press in our country was established in Pilsen around 1467, followed by another in Prague. In 1468, the first Czech book, "The Trojan Chronicle," was printed at the Pilsen press. However, the books produced during that time were not as polished as the textbooks you use today; they had a rougher and less refined appearance.

However, the esteemed Daniel made remarkable advancements in the art of printing. His printing press surpassed all others in Czechia in terms of precision and quality, earning him the nickname "Archprinter." But Veleslavín was more than just a skilled printer, he was also a renowned scholar and academic. His contributions to the Czech language were unparalleled, elevating it to new heights of excellence. Whether writing, translating, reviewing, or simply printing, Veleslavín's books stood out for their abundance, richness, clarity, and overall superiority, surpassing works in other languages just as gold outshines other metals in value. Aspiring Czech writers were advised to read Veleslavín's works as a foundation for improving their own style.

Veleslavín's immortal contributions to our native language are indeed commendable. It is regrettable that his life was cut short at the age of 53 on October 18, 1599, for he had tirelessly dedicated himself to the betterment of his fellow countrymen.

New Religious Storms

In the early 16th century, a wave of religious reform swept across Europe, challenging the teachings of the Roman Catholic Church. Just as Jan Hus had emerged in Bohemia at the beginning of the 15th century, figures like Martin Luther in Saxony and John Calvin in Switzerland rose to prominence, preaching a new doctrine that deviated from Catholic beliefs. Those who embraced Luther's teachings formed the Evangelical Church, while followers of Calvin established the Reformed Church. Catholics referred to both groups as Protestants, a term that originated from their protestation at the Diet of Speyer in 1529, where they voiced opposition to the decision to restrict access to the Holy Mass and demanded a postponement until a general church council could be convened.

The situation in Bohemia was unique. There existed a significant faction among the Catholics who sympathized with Luther's ideas. The Taborites, now known as the Czech Brethren, aligned themselves with the Reformed Church.

Although this displeased the Czech kings, they tolerated it to prevent further unrest. Emperor Rudolf II, known for his patronage of science and art, even granted the Czech Brethren a special document called the Letter of Majesty, which allowed them to construct churches and prayer houses on their estates. The Protestants built churches in Broumov and Hrob. However, the Broumov church belonged to the abbot of Broumov, who ordered its closure. Likewise, the Archbishop of Prague, who owned the Hrob estate, ordered the demolition of the Hrob church. These actions outraged the Protestants, prompting them to file a lawsuit against Emperor Matthias, who had ascended to the Bohemian throne in 1611, seeking protection for the people of Broumov and Hrob and the preservation of their religious freedom. In response, the imperial authorities declared that both churches were demolished by imperial decree and warned of severe punishments for those who had protested. Upon hearing this, the Protestants grew restless, murmuring their discontent and making threats against the officials. Fearing disturbances, the Catholics took refuge in their homes, locking themselves away.

On May 23, 1618, just before Ascension Day, the Protestant estates assembled at Prague Castle, armed and seeking retaliation against their adversaries. At nine o'clock, they forcefully entered the chamber where the four imperial regents, Adam of Šternberk, William Slavata,

Jaroslav of Martinice, and Matthew DePolt of Lobkowicz, were present. Accusing them of various alleged misdeeds, they singled out Šternberk and Lobkowicz, who were not their enemies, and escorted them out of the room. Vilém of Lobkowicz addressed Martinice and Slavata, stating, "We do not regard you as regents, but as public enemies who disrupt the peace." Václav V. of Roupov added, "Well, then let's handle them accordingly. Later, we will present a defense to demonstrate to the world that our actions were just and righteous. It is time to put an end to these archenemies." In a shocking act, they attacked Martinice and threw him out of the window, followed by Slavata. Fabricius Platter, their secretary, also suffered the same fate. Miraculously, none of them perished as they landed on a heap of refuse beneath the window. Fabricius was the first to recover and hastened to Vienna to inform the emperor about the incident.

Simultaneously, the non-Catholic estates formed an alliance among themselves, electing thirty directors or high administrators to govern and safeguard the Kingdom of Bohemia. They assumed control of the royal revenues and began assembling troops. The estates of Moravia and Silesia joined their cause. Upon learning of these developments, Emperor Matthias grew furious and vowed severe punishment for those responsible for the disorder. This marked the commencement of a protracted conflict that turned our nation into a true martyr, known as the Thirty Years' War (1618-1648). However, prior to the outbreak of war, Emperor Matthias passed away, and his uncle, Ferdinand of Styria, ascended to the Bohemian throne.

Battle of White Mountain

Immediately following his accession to the throne, Ferdinand II reached out to the Czech estates, urging them to cease their hostilities and uphold peace. He assured them that he would uphold their rights and freedoms if they heeded his plea. However, the Protestant faction disregarded his words, fueled by their deep animosity towards Ferdinand due to his staunch Catholic beliefs. They swiftly assembled an army and launched an assault on the royal palace in Vienna, demanding that the emperor acquiesce to their demands. Yet Ferdinand adamantly refused to sign any agreements.

In a subsequent development, Ferdinand was elected as the King of Germany in Frankfurt on the Main. Meanwhile, representatives from the Czech, Moravian, Silesian, and Lusatian estates congregated in Prague and selected a different monarch for themselves - Frederick, the Elector Palatine, who embraced the Reformed faith. Upon Frederick's arrival in Prague, he was ceremoniously crowned as the King of Bohemia amidst grandeur and splendor.

Regrettably, this election would prove ill-fated. Frederick proved to be a feeble and inadequate ruler, prioritizing indulgence and revelry over his responsibilities. He failed to embody the essence of a true king, instead acting as a conqueror. He pillaged Catholic churches, desecrated altars, paintings, sculptures, and other sacred artifacts, confiscating them and transporting them to his own realm. Furthermore, Frederick served as the leader of a league comprising Protestant German princes known as the Union of Evangelical Unity. In response, Catholic princes formed their own coalition named the Holy League, with Maximilian, the Duke of Bavaria, at its helm.

However, this period of stability was short-lived. In the early months of 1620, Ferdinand instigated a war against Frederick, calling upon the aid of the Poles, Spaniards, Italians, and Maximilian's seasoned league, which possessed considerable military experience and led the main army. Once Austria was subdued, Ferdinand shifted his focus to Bohemia, successfully capturing Krumlov, České Budějovice, and Prachatice. Písek, a city that valiantly resisted, suffered severe retribution, prompting other cities to surrender voluntarily to avoid a similar fate. The leaders of Frederick's army, Anhalt and Hohenlohe, supported by Bohemians, proved to be ineffective and timid in battle, constantly retreating and shying away from confrontation. It wasn't until the Battle of White Mountain, situated on a plain to the west of Prague, that they finally made a stand and fortified themselves with trenches. In due course, Maximilian arrived on the scene, setting the stage for a decisive clash on November 8, 1620, a fateful Sunday.

The battle commenced, and cries of anguish echoed through the air. But where was Frederick during this crucial moment? He was reveling and enjoying himself within the walls of Prague Castle. Suddenly, a messenger burst into his presence, urgently conveying the news that the battle had commenced and imploring the king to hasten to the aid of his troops. However, by the time Frederick reached the gate, the German and Bohemian forces had already fled from the battlefield. Only the Czech and Moravian soldiers, under the leadership of Thurn and Šlik, valiantly resisted and fought with unwavering determination. The battlefield was strewn with the lifeless bodies of 6,000 fallen soldiers. Witnessing the devastating defeat, the ineffectual Frederick fled with his wife and children to Wrocław. Due to the brevity of his reign, lasting just a single winter, he would forever be known as the "Winter King."

Following the defeat, the citizens of Prague yielded to Maximilian, granting him access to the city gates. He and his forces seized a vast array of treasures and priceless artifacts, loading them onto over 1,500 carts bound for Bavaria. Karl of Liechtenstein was then dispatched to establish law and order, delivering justice and punishment in the name of the triumphant emperor. On June 21, 1621, in Prague's Old Town Square, twenty-seven lords and knights, identified as the instigators of the rebellion, faced the grim fate of death by beheading. Others faced different forms of punishment, including floggings, property confiscation, lifelong imprisonment, or expulsion from the country. In total, 36,000 families, among them 1,088 noble and knightly households, along with numerous scholars, were compelled to abandon their cherished homeland of Bohemia.

It was an era filled with profound sorrow and anguish for our nation. The people were coerced into converting to Catholicism, and those who resisted faced severe consequences. The properties of those who departed or were penalized were predominantly seized by foreigners, many of whom harbored enmity towards our people. To extinguish any enlightenment, the Jesuits, who held control over educational institutions, resorted to burning Czech books, leaving our populace bereft of intellectual illumination.

John Amos Comenius

Jan Amos Komenský was born in the picturesque town of Uherský Brod in Moravia. Towards the end of the 16th century, he tragically lost his parents, and his guardian neglected his care, allowing young Amos to wander freely. Despite the temptations of the world and the influence of unscrupulous companions, Amos remained steadfast and incorruptible. At the age of 16, he embarked on his educational journey. Upon completing his studies, he served as a rector at various schools in Moravia. However, due to his non-Catholic faith, he, like many others, was compelled to leave his homeland and seek exile abroad. He found refuge in Poland and settled in Leszno, where he was warmly embraced by the people who elected him as the superintendent of schools and the highest priest. Word of his exceptional erudition spread throughout Europe, making him a sought-after figure. He possessed a remarkable aptitude for school administration and the art of teaching children.

The Swedish king extended an invitation to Komenský, requesting his assistance in the improvement and elevation of Swedish schools. Likewise, he received letters from England, inviting him to assume the role of superintendent of English schools. Komenský spent some time in both Sweden and England, leaving a lasting impact. After his return to Poland, the Duke of Ziębice invited him to visit and help establish schools in the region. Driven by the same purpose, Amos embarked on journeys to Silesia, Brandenburg, the city of Hamburg, and ultimately, Amsterdam. Why was he in such high demand everywhere he went?

Komenský was a distinguished and profoundly learned man. His contributions to humanity are immense and extend to various nations, including Czechs, Slovaks, French, English, Germans, and beyond. His influence on their educational systems is widely admired, earning him the title of the father of schools in Central Europe. You, dear children, have much to be grateful for to him. In the past, learning was a challenging and arduous endeavor, but thanks to Komenský's advancements in education, every child now has the opportunity to learn in a more accessible and enjoyable manner, acquiring knowledge and experiencing the beauty of subjects previously untapped. Komenský was also a prolific writer, leaving behind numerous remarkable works in both Latin and the Czech language. Among his most renowned pieces are "Didactics," "The Labyrinth of the World and the Paradise of the Heart," and "Orbis Pictus." He stands as one of the most extraordinary Czech writers. However, he did not find his final rest in Bohemia or Moravia. Instead, he passed away in exile, in the city of Amsterdam, where he was laid to rest in 1671.

"Those who lead a virtuous life weave a wreath of glory for themselves."

Albrecht von Wallenstein

Albrecht z Valdštejna hailed from an esteemed Czech noble family. Even in his youth, his passion for the military was evident. Toy soldiers held more allure for him than any other game, but only if he could assume the role of commander. As he matured, he enlisted in the army and pledged his allegiance to Czech King Ferdinand II. Through his exceptional courage, Wallenstein rapidly ascended the ranks, earning a distinguished reputation as a military leader.

During that era, as we have previously learned, a war raged between the Protestant princes united under the Evangelical Union and the Catholic princes forming the League. This conflict served as an extension of the religious strife that originated in Prague. Seeking aid, the Protestants invited Christian IV, the King of Denmark, to join their cause. Ferdinand, faced with financial constraints, encountered significant challenges in combating this formidable adversary. It was then that Wallenstein made a momentous offer—he would independently raise an army and take up arms against the enemy. Eagerly, Ferdinand granted him the necessary authorization. News of Wallenstein's recruitment efforts spread like wildfire, attracting both locals and foreigners to his camp. Soon, his forces swelled to an impressive 100,000 men. With this formidable army, he swiftly advanced across German lands, swiftly securing dominion over the Baltic coast. His ambitions even extended to seizing control of Denmark itself. However, peace was brokered between Christian and Ferdinand in 1629. In recognition of Wallenstein's instrumental role, the emperor bestowed upon him the Duchy of Friedland in northern Bohemia, along with nine cities, 57 castles, and numerous villages. Additionally, he received the Duchy of Mecklenburg in Germany, which he had successfully conquered. Subsequently, he disbanded his army.

From that point onward, Wallenstein adopted the life of a private citizen, residing in his magnificent palace in Prague's Lesser Town. His illustrious court garnered widespread renown, characterized not only by the grandeur of its lord but also by the splendor exhibited by its servants.

Meanwhile, the Protestants reached out to Gustavus Adolphus, the king of Sweden, seeking assistance. With unwavering determination, he arrived in Germany at the helm of a small yet resolute army. Fortunes favored his cause as he vanquished the Catholic forces one after another, propelling his ally John George, the Elector of Saxony, into Bohemia. John George swiftly seized Prague, claiming whatever spoils pleased him, and transporting them back to Saxony in a caravan of over 50 wagons.

Emperor Ferdinand, confronted with dire circumstances once again, realized the need for a stalwart champion and turned to the indomitable Wallenstein. Acting swiftly, he entrusted Wallenstein with the task of assembling a fresh army to vanquish the enemy. To everyone's astonishment, as soon as Wallenstein rallied his troops, warriors from all directions rallied under his victorious banners. First, he confronted the Saxons, expelling them from the land. He then set his sights on Gustavus Adolphus, leading to the momentous Battle of Lützen in what is now Prussian Saxony, in the year 1632.

King Gustavus Adolphus commanded a force of 20,000 men, while Wallenstein mustered a meager 12,000. Neither side could claim outright victory, but the clash was unforgettable. Tragically, Gustavus Adolphus met his demise, bringing an end to the battle. Wallenstein emerged triumphant in several encounters against the Protestants, capturing numerous cities that instilled great fear in his adversaries.

However, his fortunes soon took a turn for the worse as he fell out of favor with the emperor.

Manipulated by some of his adversaries, the emperor came to believe that Wallenstein had conspired with the enemy and harbored ambitions of becoming the king of Bohemia. Consequently, Wallenstein was branded a traitor, and Gallas assumed the role of supreme military commander. A courageous leader of the imperial forces named Piccolomini was entrusted with the task of apprehending Wallenstein, who was eventually handed over to the emperor. Meanwhile, with a small army at his disposal, Wallenstein made a strategic move from Pilsen to Cheb.

Tragedy befell Wallenstein during a banquet held in Cheb, where all his friends were mercilessly slain. Late into the night, a captain burst into Wallenstein's chamber, rousing him from his sleep. Confused and alarmed by the commotion, Wallenstein approached the window to assess the situation. Before he could react, the captain stormed into the room, accusing Wallenstein of betraying the imperial army and daring to seize the crown from the emperor's head. Unarmed and defenseless, Wallenstein exhibited remarkable composure as he bared his chest, opened his arms, and met his demise with a sword piercing his heart. Remarkably, he uttered not a single word. This tragic event unfolded on February 25, 1634. In the aftermath, Wallenstein's opponents claimed his vast estates for themselves.

To this day, the question of Wallenstein's guilt or innocence remains unresolved. The documents found on him made no mention of any act of treachery.

The Thirty Years War

Following the untimely demise of Wallenstein, the war waged on for another grueling fourteen years. After a series of prolonged battles, the conflict eventually returned to Bohemia. Swedish commanders like Banner, Torstenson, Wrangel, and Königsmark successively invaded our homeland, leaving a trail of devastation in their wake. They ravaged, burned, and looted, sparing no altar, and subjecting Catholic priests to cruel torment. They laid their hands on anything of value: books, manuscripts, artworks, jewels, and precious sculptures. These spoils were loaded onto ships and transported along the Elbe, bound for Sweden.

General Königsmark went so far as to launch an audacious attempt to conquer the Lesser Town and gain complete control over Prague. However, a glimmer of hope emerged when news spread that the warring factions of Osnabrück and Münster in Westphalia had signed a peace treaty in 1648. This brought about a momentous turn of events as the Swedes withdrew from Bohemia.

Nevertheless, the aftermath of the Thirty Years' War proved catastrophic. The once magnificent and prosperous land of Bohemia, renowned for its bravery and intellectual prowess, was reduced to a desolate wasteland. The Swedes had pillaged every town and village they came across, with half of the villages vanishing altogether. Most cities lay in ruins, reduced to smoldering ashes, and castles and fortresses stood as mere remnants of their former glory. The Swedish colonel Pfuhl unabashedly boasted of his cruelty, proudly claiming responsibility for the burning of eight hundred Czech villages and the decimation of their surrounding areas.

The situation in both rural and urban areas was equally dire. Fields stood abandoned, gardens empty, and livestock scarcely visible. Out of the once-thriving population of three million diligent and educated inhabitants, only around 800,000 impoverished, fearful, and forsaken souls remained. The rest had met their demise through the horrors of war – swords, flames, fear, hunger, and bitter cold. The Czech people, known for their bravery and spirit, had lost their national pride and courage, seeking refuge in forests and desolate wilderness, barely surviving or relying on charity. Even the spirit of art had faded away. The Czechs, disassociating themselves from their own identity, discarded their Slavic attire. Being called a Czech had become a source of shame!

The task of reclaiming the land was arduous for the Czechs. Often lacking proper tools, they resorted to harnessing themselves to the plow and patching up their dwellings with clay and straw. Witnessing such misery, hearts trembled in empathy. What had become of the realm once ruled by Ottokar and Charles?

Ferdinand III, who ascended to the throne of Bohemia and Germany following the passing of his father, Ferdinand II, in 1637, was deeply moved by the immense suffering. He held genuine concern for the Czech people, frequently visiting Prague, speaking in the Czech language, and offering assistance to those in need. Slowly but surely, our homeland began to heal and rebuild.

František Antonín, Count Špork

František Antonín, Count Špork, was a renowned noble of the 18th century who left a lasting impact by supporting the arts and assisting the less fortunate. Born on March 9, 1662, in Heřmanice in Chrudimsko, his passion for art began to bloom even in his youth, and he wholeheartedly dedicated himself to its pursuit. After completing his studies, he embarked on the customary travels undertaken by noble gentlemen of that era, exploring foreign lands and visiting illustrious courts, both royal and princely. Along his journeys, he meticulously documented everything he found valuable, beautiful, and artistically significant.

Having acquired a wealth of knowledge and experiences, he returned to his homeland, where his reputation as a learned and noble individual spread throughout the entire empire. Emperor Leopold I recognized his capabilities and appointed him as his chamberlain, then later as his deputy in Bohemia, and eventually as his privy counselor. However, these esteemed positions only served to fuel Špork's diligence and zeal rather than engender pride within him. He believed that with his elevated responsibilities, he had a greater duty to do good in the world. Remaining true to this noble principle, he sought opportunities to bring about positive change wherever and whenever possible.

Understanding the significance of education and personal growth in advancing the well-being of a nation, Špork ensured that Czech youth had access to exceptional teachers who would impart knowledge and virtues. He corresponded with renowned artists and scholars across Europe, sending them letters with gifts or expressing kindness and praise to win their favor. Importing valuable and exquisite books from various countries, particularly France, he enriched his three libraries located in Prague, Lysá, and Kukus, making them available for lending to the public. Recognizing that his countrymen were not particularly inclined towards reading, he endeavored to cultivate their interest in a different manner. He personally financed a thriving printing press in Lysá and had the best moral and educational books translated from other languages, printing them to be distributed freely among his fellow countrymen.

As a compassionate and benevolent lord, he exhibited special care for the impoverished, offering generous alms to them each day. During the widespread famine of 1695, he opened his granaries and distributed a substantial amount of grain among those in need. Within his estates, he established hospitals to provide for the elderly, ensuring they received significant pensions. To this day, one such hospital in Kukus supports a hundred residents, both men and women, while a compassionate monastery of twelve brothers accompanies it. Monasteries were also erected in Lysá and Hradiště Chůstnikově, where he generously contributed large sums of money. The Retirement Home in Prague received a remarkable donation of 60,000 gold coins from him. His compassion extended not only to the needy in Bohemia but also to innocent individuals suffering in foreign lands. Deeply moved by the plight of Christians in Turkish captivity, he bestowed a hundred thousand gold coins upon the Trinitarian priests. He instructed them to allocate two-thirds of the interest towards the ransom of captive Christians and the remaining one-third for the liberation of unfortunate citizens imprisoned in Prague due to debts.

Yet, even this noble benefactor faced adversaries! Treacherous individuals rose against him, entangling him in numerous disputes regarding his wealth. One of his opponents even obtained an arrest warrant, capturing him at Lysá Castle during a fateful night in 1728. Subsequently, this great benefactor of our homeland found himself imprisoned in Prague's Daliborka Tower. The Episcopal Consistory of Hradec Králové accused him of disseminating heretical books and housing them within the Kukus library.

Thirty thousand books from his library were loaded onto wagons and transported to Hradec Králové. The investigation into these books spanned seven long years, ultimately leading to the complete recognition of Špork's innocence in 1736. The books were returned to him, and the informers were obliged to publicly apologize to him in Kukus.

Count Špork carried his burden with patience and continued to lead a quiet life, unwavering in his commitment to doing good, even to those who wronged him. However, it was not long thereafter, on March 30, 1738, that he passed away, leaving behind a legacy of righteousness. Although the world may not have fully appreciated his kindness, surely God, whose gaze delves into the depths of every heart and soul, had prepared abundant rewards for him in the heavenly realm.

Karel Skřeta and Petr Brandi

Three hundred years ago, lived the esteemed painters Karel Škreta and Petr Brandi. Karel Škreta, born around 1604 in Prague, hailed from the respected Šotnovský family of Závořice. He received his education in Prague and soon devoted himself to the art of painting. When the tumultuous Thirty Years' War erupted in Bohemia, he embarked on a journey to Italy. As you may have heard, artists, particularly painters and sculptors, often ventured to Italy to marvel at the masterful and breathtaking works created by the most renowned artists the world had ever known. Italy boasted grand cities like Venice, Bologna, Florence, and above all, Rome, where numerous magnificent paintings were displayed. Škreta spent an extended period there, diligently immersing himself in the timeless creations of the most celebrated Italian painters. He also visited prestigious art schools, and his talent flourished to such an extent that his fame quickly spread throughout Italy. The people of Bologna even approached him, asking him to become a teacher at their art academy, but Škreta humbly declined the offer and returned to his beloved homeland.

Emperor Ferdinand III and the Czech nobility bestowed upon him numerous prestigious commissions. None of our Czech painters could rival his exceptional skill, and many were envious of his remarkable talent.

At one point, a certain nobleman commissioned a painting from Škreta. In the style of the illustrious Italian painter Carracci, Škreta meticulously created the artwork. However, this prejudiced nobleman disparaged anything originating from our country, as if no one in Bohemia possessed any talent or understanding. He scorned Škreta's painting and dismissively sent it back. Although this criticism deeply wounded Škreta, he persevered. He discreetly signed his name in a corner of the painting and dispatched it to Italy, where it was recognized as a work by Carracci. Oh, several years later, the same nobleman traveled to Italy and, after paying a hefty price in Florence, acquired the very same painting. He then sent it to Škreta, requesting that he create a copy. However, Škreta astoundingly embarrassed the nobleman by pointing out his own name on the painting. Overwhelmed with shame, the nobleman underwent a change of heart and thereafter praised Škreta's art. To this day, Škreta's paintings grace homes, churches, and palaces. Unfortunately, in 1674, death claimed him, putting an end to his illustrious contributions to the art world.

Another remarkable Czech painter, Petr Brandi, was born in Prague in 1660. Even as a young boy, he found delight in sketching various figures and buildings. During his school days, while other restless students engaged in conversation and play, he would immerse himself in drawing. Whether it was using chalk on a slate or a pencil in his notebook, he would diligently create his artwork. At the age of 15, he left school to fully commit himself to painting, a pursuit that brought him immense joy. For four years, he studied under the guidance of Jan Šroter. Subsequently, he painstakingly imitated the exceptional paintings of the most renowned masters and meticulously captured scenes from nature.

His works stood out for their vibrant colors and vivid depictions. He demonstrated remarkable skill in portraits and religious paintings, which can be found in abundance within Czech churches, chapels, and the private collections of affluent nobles. Tragically, in 1739, he passed away in Kutná Hora, living in great poverty. Despite his destitution, his funeral was a grand affair, with numerous priests, the city council, and 300 miners accompanying him to his final resting place. Many years have elapsed since then, but his paintings continue to be highly sought after and revered.

Marie Theresa

The love of subjects is the most precious treasure of monarchs.

−Emperor Albert II.

In the year 1740, Marie Theresa ascended to power, assuming control over the hereditary lands of Austria. With a heart of compassion, she tended to the welfare of her beloved subjects, contemplating ways to enhance and fortify prosperity throughout her domains.

The protracted conflicts, in which both her predecessors and she herself were embroiled, notably against the ambitious Frederick II, the King of Prussia, demanded significant expenditures. State revenues fell short of these costs. Contemplating this challenge, she had a brilliant idea that the advancement of agriculture, industry, and the diligent work ethic of her prosperous subjects could serve as a plentiful source of prosperity for each individual and a substantial means to address the empire's needs. From that point onward, she bolstered agriculture, promoted mining, encouraged commerce and industry, and established sizable factories and workshops. In doing so, she prioritized the material well-being of her subjects.

However, the happiness of a nation and a state extends beyond mere material prosperity. Marie Theresa swiftly recognized this and ardently dedicated herself to the intellectual education of her people. She fostered a more comprehensive and extensive approach to nurturing and educating the younger generation.

Although there were schools in towns and select villages where children received education in religious matters and essential life knowledge, these schools remained insufficient. To address this, Marie Theresa issued a decree for the establishment of at least one national school in every parish district. She entrusted knowledgeable individuals with developing the educational guidelines for these schools. In Vienna and other major cities within her domain, she established exemplary primary schools, where exceptional teachers not only imparted knowledge but also served as role models for younger educators. She urged her subjects to diligently send their children to school between the ages of six and twelve. While this was commendable, a flaw existed in the requirement that only the German language be taught in all schools. This hindered the good intentions for those who spoke different languages, as the children struggled to comprehend the lessons. It was primarily her son, Joseph II, who believed that linguistic unity among the Austrian nations could be achieved by adopting German as the common language, with the assistance of specific individuals.

Marie Theresa's efforts were blessed by God. State revenues experienced significant growth, facilitated by more comprehensive tax collection. These tax funds were then redistributed in a wiser manner, taking into account each individual's wealth to alleviate excessive burdens on the less affluent. The hardships of serfdom were eased, and greater freedoms were granted to the people. As a result, everyone willingly contributed their taxes, understanding that it ultimately served their own well-being.

After a benevolent reign of 40 years, Marie Theresa passed away in 1780.

Joseph II

Emperor Joseph II was an incredibly noble ruler who held the well-being of his subjects as his highest priority. He diligently traveled throughout the empire, ensuring that laws were upheld, order was maintained, and the pursuit of happiness was facilitated. His particular focus was on improving the conditions of the peasantry. In his efforts, he abolished serfdom, granting freedom of movement between social classes. During a visit to Moravia in 1769, near the village of Rousinov, he encountered a peasant plowing in the fields. Struck by empathy and curiosity, he ordered his carriage to halt, disembarked, and requested to plow a few furrows himself. The peasant respectfully bowed to the unknown gentleman, handed him the plow, and took the reins to guide the oxen.

Together, they worked side by side, plowing furrows. After a brief moment, the unknown gentleman unbuttoned his coat. The peasant, taken aback, noticed a golden star on the gentleman's chest. Before the peasant could recover, the unknown gentleman revealed his true identity, declaring, "I am Joseph, your emperor and father!" Deeply moved by the encounter, the emperor generously rewarded the peasant. When the harvest season arrived, the humble Moravian peasant gathered the grain harvested from the furrows plowed by the emperor and presented it as a gift to him in Vienna. Delighted by this heartfelt gesture, the emperor accepted the gift with joy and reciprocated the peasant's generosity. To forever commemorate this act, which showcased the emperor's noble regard for the farming class, a significant stone monument was erected in the very field where he plowed, bearing the inscription: "On this field, Joseph II, German Emperor, plowed."

Joseph II also implemented the Tolerance Patent, a significant act that granted religious freedom to non-Catholics. As a result, the Jesuit Order was dissolved, and in 1781, Joseph himself disbanded numerous monasteries, allowing only those engaged in educational or healthcare endeavors to continue their operations.

This visionary emperor pursued numerous reforms and innovations, but his ambitious pace led to many failures. Tragically, Joseph II's life was cut short, as he passed away prematurely in 1790.

Emperor Francis I

Emperor Francis I also faced his share of challenges during a tumultuous era marked by numerous wars. It was a time when the French people revolted against their rulers, condemning and executing their own king. They not only declared war on neighboring monarchs but also advocated for their subjects to overthrow their own rulers and govern themselves. However, the Austrian people held deep affection for their benevolent leader and remained steadfastly loyal. Rather than siding with the French, they bravely marched into battle against them. Unfortunately, the French possessed an exceptional leader at the time, none other than Napoleon. His military prowess was unmatched, and victory seemed to follow him wherever he went. He achieved multiple triumphs over the Austrian army, leaving even foreign nations in awe of his capabilities. The French celebrated his leadership and even elected him as their emperor.

As emperor, Napoleon waged constant wars, driven by an ambition to conquer the entire world. He defeated Emperor Francis, ravaging his lands and seizing control of certain territories. He regarded himself as unequalled, a supreme ruler with the power to do as he pleased. Yet, God opposes the proud and bestows His grace upon the humble. Emperor Alexander of Russia and King Frederick William III of Prussia united forces against Napoleon, with Emperor Francis joining their alliance. Together, they outnumbered Napoleon three to one and emerged victorious, stripping him of his empire and exiling him to the island of Elba.

However, Napoleon's subsequent return and attempted restoration of his emperorship led to another confrontation, with Emperor Francis once again leading the charge alongside his allies. Napoleon was eventually captured and banished to the remote island of St. Helena, situated in the vast Atlantic Ocean between Africa and America. In the aftermath, European monarchs gathered in Vienna to convene meetings and restore the territories conquered by Napoleon to their rightful owners. Thus, peace and order were restored to Europe, and Emperor Francis continued to reign happily for many years, ensuring stability within his empire.

Ferninand I

After Francis, his son Ferdinand I ascended the throne, assuming the title of Ferdinand V as the King of Bohemia. His reign witnessed remarkable prosperity as trade thrived, industries expanded, railways and chain bridges were constructed throughout the Austrian lands, and steam navigation was actively promoted.

However, in 1848, a revolt erupted in France, spreading across various countries, including Austria. During this period, the Czech estates voiced their demand for the emperor to convene an extraordinary assembly, aiming to address necessary reforms. A group of Czech intellectuals further appealed for the restoration of equal status for the Czech language alongside German in schools and government offices within the Kingdom of Bohemia. They also advocated for the Crown Lands of Bohemia, Moravia, and Silesia to have a united assembly representing not only the higher estates but also the common populace. Their aspirations encompassed granting greater autonomy to municipalities, the abolition of serfdom with fair compensation, and other similar requests echoed by other regions within the empire.

The emperor made a promise to grant a constitution to his nations, indicating his intention to share the supreme legislative power with elected deputies and representatives of the estates in the future.

This pledge ignited uprisings in various regions, including Lombardy, Venice, Vienna, Hungary, and eventually Prague. In Prague, the populace clashed with the army led by Prince Windischgrätz, resulting in the city being subjected to artillery fire and eventual surrender. Regrettably, these disturbances prematurely disrupted a crucial endeavor in its early stages. The "Slavic Congress," inaugurated on June 2, 1848, on Žofín Island in Prague, was notably interrupted, and the progress of the constitutional assembly for the Czech lands was hindered.

Due to his ailing health, Emperor Ferdinand abdicated his imperial position on December 1, 1848, passing the mantle to his cousin, Francis Joseph, who was the son of Archduke Francis Charles.

František Josef I

After assuming the hereditary throne of Austria, František Josef I wasted no time in instituting new imperial offices and courts, along with distinct economic, industrial, and trade chambers for each region. The education system underwent significant transformations, including the establishment of vocational schools, and the utilization of the Czech language in elementary schools across the Czech lands.

However, Minister Bach later reversed these liberal reforms, curtailed local self-government, and pursued a policy of Germanization, aiming to assimilate our nation as much as possible. Under his leadership, Austria suffered the loss of Lombardy and incurred substantial financial setbacks during the Eastern War.

In response, on October 20, 1860, the emperor issued a decree reinstating a free constitution within the empire, a right previously granted to his nations by Ferdinand. This heralds the dawn of a more promising era for us. Let us pray to God that He never abandons our nation, as His presence has been constant throughout our history, guiding us through trials and great disasters, ultimately leading us back to a resplendent existence.

Renaissance of Czech Literature

Emperor Joseph II pursued a vision of unifying all Austrian lands under a single rule and thus promoted the use of the German language in offices and schools. However, this approach encountered resistance and led to a backlash. The Czech people, weary of Germanization, embraced their diminishing mother tongue and dedicated themselves tirelessly to its revival. This movement gained particular momentum during the reign of Francis I, who declared himself Emperor of Austria and relinquished the German crown in 1806.

Czech literature had already blossomed during the era of the Přemyslid dynasty. In the 13th century, an impressive collection of poetry emerged, with some works dating back to ancient pagan antiquity. The precious remnants of these compositions, preserved in the Königinhof manuscript, serve as a testament to that era. Additionally, numerous legends, religious stories, chronicles, and other writings from the same period have endured.

Among the notable legends is that of St. Catherine. The Czech language achieved even greater heights during the Luxembourg dynasty. At that time, Czechs excelled in both physical and intellectual prowess, diligently nurturing sciences and the arts within our homeland. Education spread widely from our country's shores. In the 15th century, the Czech language commanded great respect. It was not only used at the Czech royal court but also served as a noble and courtly language in the courts of Hungary, Poland, and Lithuania. Its prestige reached its zenith during the reign of Rudolf II, a staunch patron of science who invited the most erudite minds to Prague. No other nation could boast such exceptional schools and scholars as our beloved homeland.

The Czech language became the predominant tongue throughout the kingdom, spoken at the royal court, in the assemblies of the estates, in courts, and employed in all official documents, schools, and churches.

However, the situation in Bohemia took a turn after the Battle of White Mountain. While the Czech and German languages were officially granted equal rights, in practice, German was favored, while Czech faced oppression. The expulsion and decline of many prominent Czech noble families led to the influx of German nobility into Bohemia. Czech books were burned, German schools were established, and German became the dominant language in administration. The Czech nation, once vibrant and proud, found itself stripped of its spirit and relegated to a lesser position. Bearing the name "Czech" became a source of shame for many.

Yet, under the reign of Francis I, a new era dawned upon us. A host of learned individuals embraced our rich language and dedicated themselves to its enrichment. Remarkably, the emperor himself not only approved but actively supported their noble endeavors. Francis went as far as mandating the teaching of Czech in Latin schools and insisting that imperial officials attain proficiency in the language (in 1816 and 1818, respectively). He also gave his endorsement to the National Czech Museum, which aimed to foster Czech-Slavic education, and supported the Czech Mother Society, dedicated to publishing high-quality Czech literature and books. These actions signified a resurgence of pride and appreciation for our language and culture.

Following his admirable example, numerous noble and affluent individuals such as the Counts and Princes of Kolowrat, Lobkowitz, Kinský, and others, alongside Wenceslaus Tham, Václav Hanka, Sychra, Milota Zdir, Polák, Ladislav Čelakovský, Karel Sabina, Vítězslav Hálek, Ján Kollár, Václav Kliment Klicpera, Jan Svatopluk Presl, Jaroslav Langer, Jan Pravoslav Koubek,

Josef Kajetán Tyl, Karel Havlíček, Josef Franta Šnajdr, Bedřich Smetana, Jan Evangelista Purkyně, Karel Vinařický, František Vacek (Kamenický), Karel Jaromír Erben, František Ladislav Čelakovský, Karel Jaromír Erben, Karel Václav Jireček, Jan Erazim Bílý, Jan Karel Skořepa, Alois Vojtěch Šembera, Jan Palacký, Karel Tieftrunk, Josef Erben, Josef Wenig, Gustav Pfleger, Bohumil Janda (Cidlinský), Emanuel Tonner, Vincenc Brandl, Jan Lepař, Josef Emler, František Sakař, František Václav Jeřábek, Vítězslav Hájek, Jiljí Vrat. Jahn, Jan Neruda, Karolina Světlá, Zofie Podlipská, Eliška Krásnohorská, Věnceslav Lužický, and many others have achieved renown and made significant contributions to scholarship and literature.

We take great pride in witnessing the resurgence of our nation, where under the Austrian flag, many nations excel in education, surpassing others and standing as the most knowledgeable and gifted among all Slavic nations.

Behold, dear Czechs, the triumphant legacy of our ancestors! They achieved greatness not only on the battlefield but also in the realms of arts and sciences. Their victories came with ease, yet they remained devoted to the pursuit of peace. During times of tranquility, they nurtured the sciences and arts, leaving an indelible impact not just on our compatriots, but on the entire world. Thus, we and foreigners alike hold our illustrious ancestors in high esteem, speaking their names with utmost reverence. Above all, let us cherish our ancestors and the language they bestowed upon us.

To feel ashamed of one's language is to invite the disdain of all humanity.

The Bohemian Revival

The Bohemian Revival, also known as the Czech National Revival, was a cultural and intellectual movement that emerged in the late 18th century, leaving a lasting impact on Czech society. It was a response to the diminishing state of Czech culture and national identity caused by Germanization policies and the dominance of the German language in official spheres.

Driven by a deep sense of national pride, the revival movement aimed to preserve and revive the Czech language, history, and cultural heritage. Its objective was to restore the Czech language as a means of communication, education, and cultural expression. The movement sought to reclaim the Czech identity and promote the concept of a distinct Czech nation within the diverse Habsburg Empire.

Prominent figures such as Josef Dobrovský, Josef Jungmann, and František Palacký played pivotal roles in shaping the Bohemian Revival. They devoted themselves to the study and standardization of the Czech language, striving to elevate it to the status of a literary language and encourage its usage in literature, education, and administration. Their efforts resulted in the development of new vocabulary, grammar rules, and dictionaries that contributed to the enrichment and codification of the Czech language.

The revivalists of the Bohemian Revival also recognized the importance of preserving the Czech historical heritage through the collection and publication of historical documents and manuscripts. Their efforts aimed to uncover and safeguard Czech history, folklore, and traditions, fostering a deep sense of national pride and cultural continuity among the Czech people.

Beyond language and literature, the Bohemian Revival encompassed a wide range of cultural and artistic domains. It permeated music, visual arts, theater, and architecture. Renowned composers such as Bedřich Smetana and Antonín Dvořák drew inspiration from Czech folk music, incorporating its essence into their compositions and contributing to the evolution of a distinct Czech musical style.

The establishment of educational institutions played a pivotal role in the success of the revival movement, with the University of Prague being a notable example. These institutions became vital platforms for intellectual exchange, the dissemination of knowledge, and the training of a new generation of Czech scholars, writers, and leaders, ensuring the continuation and growth of the Bohemian Revival's influence.

The Bohemian Revival served as a precursor to the subsequent Czech nationalist movements and played a pivotal role in shaping the Czechoslovak independence movement of the 20th century. It nurtured a strong sense of national awareness, cultural pride, and solidarity among the Czech populace, asserting a unique Czech identity within the diverse Habsburg Empire.

In essence, the Bohemian Revival marked a significant turning point in Czech history, reinvigorating the Czech language, culture, and national identity. Its impact is still evident in modern Czech society, where the Czech language and cultural heritage continue to flourish, carrying forward the rich legacy of the Bohemian Revival.

Czechoslovak Declaration of Independence

The Czechoslovak declaration of independence in 1918 stands as a momentous event in Czech and Slovak history, signifying the birth of an independent Czechoslovak state subsequent to the dissolution of the Austro-Hungarian Empire in the aftermath of World War I.

On October 28, 1918, in the vibrant city of Prague, located in the heart of Bohemia, Czechoslovak politicians and leaders, including Tomáš Garrigue Masaryk, Milan Rastislav Štefánik, and Edvard Beneš, officially proclaimed the establishment of an independent Czechoslovakia.

This declaration marked the culmination of years of determined political and nationalistic endeavors by Czech and Slovak leaders who sought self-determination and unity. Their vision was to forge a cohesive nation that would safeguard the rights and freedoms of all citizens, irrespective of their nationality or ethnicity.

The formation of Czechoslovakia was a response to the disintegration of the Austro-Hungarian Empire and the aspiration to construct a new democratic state that would unite the Czechs and Slovaks, who shared a common language and cultural heritage. The declaration also aimed to address the aspirations of other ethnic groups within the region, including the Ruthenians and Germans.

Central to the declaration were principles of democracy, equality, and self-governance. It firmly asserted the Czechoslovak people's right to determine their own political destiny and to administer their affairs in accordance with democratic principles. Additionally, it called for the establishment of a national assembly and the implementation of a democratic constitution.

The Czechoslovak declaration of independence in 1918 stands as a pivotal moment in Czech and Slovak history, deeply influenced by the international context of the time. The disintegration of the Austro-Hungarian Empire and the conclusion of World War I created a favorable climate for the emergence of new states. Notably, the Allies, including France and the United States, actively supported the establishment of an independent Czechoslovakia and officially recognized it as a sovereign nation.

With the proclamation of independence, concerted efforts were undertaken to consolidate the nascent state and establish its governing institutions. Tomáš Garrigue Masaryk assumed the role of the first president of Czechoslovakia, while a provisional government was swiftly formed. The country embarked on a transformative phase of nation-building, dedicating itself to political, social, and economic reforms.

The Czechoslovak declaration of independence in 1918 holds profound significance as a landmark event that shaped the course of Czech and Slovak history. It laid the groundwork for the establishment of an autonomous and democratic state, which would go on to play a significant role in the political, economic, and cultural development of the region. The declaration exemplified the aspirations and ideals of the Czech and Slovak people, their longing for self-determination, and their unwavering pursuit of national identity. It continues to serve as a powerful symbol of their struggle for freedom and independence.

Tomáš Garrigue Masaryk

Tomáš Garrigue Masaryk (1850-1937) was a philosopher, sociologist, and politician whose influence in Czech history cannot be overstated. Born on March 7, 1850, in Hodonín, Moravia, a region within the Austro-Hungarian Empire, Masaryk pursued studies in philosophy, history, and natural sciences at Charles University in Prague. He furthered his education with doctoral studies in Vienna and Leipzig, cementing his reputation as a distinguished academic.

Masaryk's intellectual pursuits led him to a professorship in philosophy at Charles University, where he made remarkable contributions to the realms of sociology and philosophy of history. However, his passion for the well-being and rights of the Czech people soon drew him into the political arena. As a staunch advocate for Czech national identity, he tirelessly fought for the recognition of the Czechs and the establishment of an independent Czechoslovak state. Masaryk's advocacy was deeply rooted in democratic ideals, a commitment to human rights, and the pursuit of social justice.

During World War I, Masaryk played a pivotal role in the Czechoslovak independence movement. His tireless efforts included extensive lobbying in Europe and the United States, tirelessly seeking recognition and support for the Czechoslovak cause from Allied leaders. In 1918, with the disintegration of the Austro-Hungarian Empire, Masaryk seized the moment and proclaimed the independence of Czechoslovakia. He then assumed the position of the country's first President, guiding it through its early years of nationhood.

As President, he dedicated himself to building a democratic and inclusive nation. Masaryk was a staunch champion of democracy, civil liberties, and minority rights, advocating for the principles that form the bedrock of a just society. Throughout his presidency, he worked tirelessly to create a strong and stable state, fostering unity among diverse ethnic groups and promoting social welfare policies that aimed to uplift the lives of all citizens.

Masaryk's leadership and far-sighted vision left an indelible mark on Czechoslovakia. He recognized the pivotal role of education, culture, and economic development in shaping a modern and progressive nation. By emphasizing these aspects, he sought to establish Czechoslovakia as a beacon of innovation and enlightenment. Furthermore,

Masaryk played a significant role in positioning Czechoslovakia as a respected member of the League of Nations, advocating for international cooperation and diplomacy to build a more harmonious world.

After serving as President for nearly two decades, Masaryk retired in 1935, but his influence and respect endured. Until his passing on September 14, 1937, in Lány, Czechoslovakia, he remained a revered figure and a tireless advocate for democratic values. Masaryk's legacy continues to resonate in Czech history, as he is remembered as a visionary leader, an unwavering defender of democracy and human rights, and an enduring symbol of Czechoslovak independence. His contributions in philosophy, sociology, and politics have had a lasting impact, shaping the foundation of the Czech Republic and inspiring generations of Czechs to tirelessly pursue freedom, justice, and a strong national identity.

Edvard Beneš

Edvard Beneš (1884-1948) was a prominent Czech politician and diplomat who played a crucial role in the establishment of Czechoslovakia as an independent state and in shaping its early years. Born on May 28, 1884, in Kožlany, Bohemia, Beneš dedicated his life to public service and democratic ideals.

Beneš served as the Foreign Minister of Czechoslovakia from 1918 to 1935 and then as the second President of Czechoslovakia from 1935 to 1938 and again in exile from 1940 to 1948. During his tenure, he worked to strengthen Czechoslovakia's international standing, negotiating alliances, and advocating for the nation's interests on the global stage.

As Foreign Minister, Beneš played a key role in drafting the Czechoslovak Constitution and the Treaty of Versailles, which affirmed the country's sovereignty and established its borders. He was a staunch advocate for human rights, social justice, and the rights of ethnic minorities, striving to promote Czechoslovakia as a democratic and progressive state.

Facing the increasing threat of Nazi Germany, Beneš navigated challenging circumstances leading up to World War II. He worked to protect Czechoslovakia's interests in the face of mounting pressure and was a steadfast defender of the nation's sovereignty.

After the German occupation of Czechoslovakia in 1939, Beneš established a government-in-exile in London. From there, he continued to represent Czechoslovakia's interests and coordinated resistance efforts against the Nazi occupation, working to maintain the legitimacy of the Czechoslovak government.

Following World War II, Beneš returned to Czechoslovakia and resumed the presidency until 1948. However, his presidency was marred by political challenges, including the rise of communism. The communist coup d'état in 1948 led to the establishment of a communist regime, abruptly ending Beneš's presidency.

Despite the difficulties and the circumstances surrounding the end of his presidency, Edvard Beneš's contributions to Czechoslovakia and his unwavering commitment to democratic principles remain significant. His diplomatic efforts, dedication to nation-building, and resistance against oppression make him an important figure in Czech history. Beneš's legacy continues to inspire those who value freedom, democracy, and the pursuit of justice.

The Munich Agreement

The Munich Agreement, signed on September 30, 1938, was a pivotal event in European history, specifically concerning Czechoslovakia and its relationship with Germany. It took place during a conference in Munich, Germany, involving the leaders of Germany, Italy, France, and the United Kingdom.

At the heart of the Munich Agreement was the fate of the Sudetenland, a region in Czechoslovakia with a predominantly ethnic German population. Adolf Hitler, the German Chancellor, demanded its annexation into Germany, citing the need to protect the rights of ethnic Germans residing there.

British Prime Minister Neville Chamberlain and French Prime Minister Édouard Daladier engaged in negotiations to find a peaceful solution and avoid a military conflict with Germany. Czechoslovakia, excluded from the conference, faced immense pressure to accept the agreement's terms.

According to the Munich Agreement, Czechoslovakia was compelled to cede the Sudetenland to Germany without its government's consent. This decision caused outrage and disappointment among Czechoslovak leaders, who felt betrayed by their allies. Nevertheless, fearing immediate German invasion and lacking support from their allies, Czechoslovakia reluctantly agreed to the terms.

The Munich Agreement is widely criticized for its policy of appeasement toward Nazi Germany. Many believed that sacrificing Czechoslovakia was an attempt by Western powers to appease Hitler and avoid a larger conflict. However, it soon became apparent that this approach only emboldened Germany and set the stage for further aggression.

The aftermath of the Munich Agreement had profound implications for Czechoslovakia. The loss of the Sudetenland weakened the country's defense capabilities and compromised its territorial integrity. It also resulted in the forced displacement of ethnic Czechs and Slovaks from the surrendered territories, along with mistreatment and discrimination against those who remained.

The Munich Agreement marked a critical turning point in European history, revealing the failure of diplomatic efforts to prevent the outbreak of World War II. It exposed the limitations of appeasement and the perils of disregarding the sovereignty and interests of smaller nations in the face of aggression.

The events surrounding the Munich Agreement continue to spark reflection and debate, underscoring the complexities of international relations and the consequences of compromising principles for short-term peace. They serve as a stark reminder of the importance of standing up to aggression, defending the rights and independence of nations, even in the face of significant challenges.

German Occupation of Czechoslovakia

The German occupation of Czechoslovakia, also known as the Protectorate of Bohemia and Moravia, took place during World War II from 1939 to 1945. It was a significant event that profoundly affected the Czechoslovak people and the country as a whole.

Beginning on March 15, 1939, German forces, led by Adolf Hitler, violated the terms of the Munich Agreement and invaded Czechoslovakia. The occupation resulted in the division of the country into two regions: the Protectorate of Bohemia and Moravia, directly controlled by Germany, and the independent Slovak State, a puppet state under German influence.

Under German occupation, Czechoslovakia endured a brutal regime characterized by repression, political persecution, and the suppression of Czech national identity. The Germans aimed to Germanize the region and quash any resistance to their rule.

The occupation authorities implemented various measures to exert control over the population. Czech institutions and organizations were dismantled, political parties were banned, and freedom of speech and assembly severely curtailed. The education system was reshaped to promote Nazi ideology, while the Czech language was marginalized in favor of German.

Jewish communities were particularly targeted during the occupation. Anti-Semitic policies were enforced, resulting in the deportation and extermination of thousands of Czech Jews in concentration camps. Jewish properties were confiscated, synagogues destroyed, and the Jewish population subjected to persecution and discrimination.

Resistance to the German occupation took various forms. Some Czechs joined underground resistance movements, such as the Czech resistance and the Communist Party of Czechoslovakia, engaging in acts of sabotage, espionage, and civil disobedience. Others participated in passive resistance, preserving Czech national identity through cultural and educational activities while resisting Germanization.

In May 1945, the German occupation of Czechoslovakia finally came to an end with the arrival of Allied forces, including Soviet and American troops. The country was liberated from

German control, and efforts were initiated to restore Czechoslovakia's independence and rebuild the nation.

The German occupation of Czechoslovakia left a lasting impact on the country. It resulted in the loss of thousands of lives, the destruction of cultural heritage, and significant social and economic upheaval. The experience of occupation and the struggle for liberation became an integral part of Czechoslovakia's national memory and identity, shaping its post-war trajectory and commitment to democracy and human rights.

Josef Gabčík

Josef Gabčík (1912-1942) was a Czechoslovak soldier and a crucial member of Operation Anthropoid, a mission aimed at assassinating high-ranking Nazi official Reinhard Heydrich. Heydrich, known for his involvement in the Holocaust, held a prominent position as the Deputy Reich Protector of Bohemia and Moravia.

On May 27, 1942, in Prague, Gabčík, along with his comrade Jan Kubiš, successfully carried out the mission. They ambushed Heydrich's car, launching an attack with firearms and a grenade. The assassination dealt a significant blow to the Nazi regime and demonstrated the Czech resistance's unwavering determination to fight against the occupying forces.

Following the attack, Gabčík and Kubiš sought refuge in a church crypt and later found sanctuary in the crypt of the Orthodox Cathedral of Saints Cyril and Methodius. However, their location was discovered by the Nazis, leading to a massive manhunt. In the face of overwhelming German forces, Gabčík, Kubiš, and their fellow resistance fighters courageously defended themselves.

Realizing that capture was inevitable and outnumbered by the enemy, Gabčík and Kubiš made the decision to take their own lives rather than be captured alive. Their sacrifice and heroism in the face of insurmountable odds became a lasting symbol of Czech resistance against Nazi tyranny.

Josef Gabčík's bravery and unwavering commitment to the cause of freedom have elevated him to an iconic status in Czech history. His selfless act of assassinating Heydrich and his readiness to sacrifice his own life for the liberation of his country are a testament to the indomitable spirit of the Czech people during World War II. Gabčík's legacy as a war hero and symbol of Czech resistance continues to inspire generations, serving as a reminder of the courage and sacrifice necessary to confront and defy oppression.

End of World War II

The conclusion of World War II in Czechoslovakia marked a significant and transformative period in the nation's history. After enduring six years of Nazi occupation, Czechoslovakia emerged from the shadows of oppression and embarked on a path of liberation and renewal.

As the Soviet Red Army advanced into Czechoslovak territory, the liberation from Nazi oppression drew closer. In 1945, the Soviet forces entered Czechoslovakia, pushing westward with the objective of freeing Prague from German control. The approaching Soviets sparked a coordinated uprising in Prague in May 1945, as Czech resistance fighters and civilians courageously fought against the occupiers. This Prague Uprising, a testament to the indomitable spirit of the Czech people, successfully drove out the Germans and liberated the city on May 9, 1945.

Shortly after, the remaining German forces in Czechoslovakia surrendered. The official surrender took place in Pilsen on May 12, 1945, symbolizing the end of German occupation in the country. Czechoslovakia was finally free from the weight of the Nazi regime, and its people could begin the process of rebuilding their nation.

However, the aftermath of the war presented new challenges for Czechoslovakia. The country lay in ruins, with infrastructure, industries, and cities devastated. The government faced the daunting task of post-war reconstruction, working to rebuild the nation's foundations and restore normalcy to the lives of its citizens. Economic and social reforms were implemented to rejuvenate the country and foster its recovery.

Yet, as Czechoslovakia emerged from the shadows of war, it found itself under the growing influence of the Soviet Union. The presence of Soviet troops increased, and over time, Czechoslovakia gradually fell under communist rule. This shift in the political landscape set the stage for a new chapter in the nation's history.

The end of World War II in Czechoslovakia brought relief from the horrors of Nazi occupation, ushering in a period of rebuilding and transformation. The Prague Uprising showcased the resilience and determination of the Czech people, laying the foundation for a future shaped by the challenges of post-war reconstruction and the evolving political dynamics in the years ahead.

Rise of Communism

The rise of communism in Czechoslovakia in 1948 marked a significant turning point in the country's history, shaping its political, social, and economic landscape for decades to come. The events leading up to the establishment of a communist regime were complex and influenced by both domestic and international factors.

In the aftermath of World War II, Czechoslovakia found itself under the control of the Soviet Union and its Red Army. The country's political climate had already been shifting, with growing support for left-wing parties, including the Communist Party of Czechoslovakia (CPC). The Soviet Union, keen on expanding its sphere of influence and ensuring communist regimes in Eastern Europe, saw an opportunity to consolidate power in Czechoslovakia.

In the years following the end of the war, political tensions escalated. The Czechoslovak government, led by President Edvard Beneš, consisted of a coalition of various political parties, including both communists and non-communists. However, ideological differences and power struggles between these factions intensified, leading to a deepening divide.

In February 1948, a crisis unfolded that would ultimately seal the fate of Czechoslovakia. The communist party, backed by the Soviet Union, launched a series of orchestrated actions to consolidate power and eliminate their political opponents. The communists accused non-communist ministers of conspiring against the state, leading to their dismissal from the government. This move effectively weakened non-communist influence and allowed the communists to gain control over key ministries and positions of power.

With the balance of power shifting in favor of the communists, they began to tighten their grip on the country. They embarked on a systematic campaign of repression, targeting political opponents, suppressing dissent, and establishing a one-party rule. Political freedoms and civil liberties were curtailed, and the communist party exerted control over the media, education, and cultural institutions. Economically, the communists implemented a centrally planned economy, nationalizing key industries and implementing collectivization in agriculture. Private enterprise and individual property rights were restricted, as the state took control over the means of production. The country became closely aligned with the Soviet Union and followed its model of socialism, adopting a command economy and emphasizing industrialization and heavy industry.

The rise of communism in Czechoslovakia had a profound impact on society. Dissent and opposition to the regime were met with harsh repression, leading to a climate of fear and conformity. Intellectuals, artists, and those who dared to express critical views faced censorship and persecution.

This period of communist rule lasted for more than four decades, until the Velvet Revolution in 1989. The communist regime left a lasting imprint on the country, with its effects felt in political institutions, social divisions, and the economy.

The rise of communism in Czechoslovakia in 1948 represented a turning point in the country's history, leading to a period of authoritarian rule and Soviet influence. It marked the beginning of a new era characterized by ideological conformity, state control, and the suppression of political freedoms. The impact of this period would reverberate through Czechoslovakia's history until the winds of change swept through the country with the Velvet Revolution, ushering in a new era of democracy and freedom.

Stalinist Era

The Stalinist Era in Czechoslovakia during the 1950s was a period marked by the implementation of repressive policies, political purges, and the consolidation of communist control under the influence of Soviet leader Joseph Stalin. Following the rise of communism in 1948, Czechoslovakia experienced a significant shift towards an authoritarian regime aligned with the Soviet Union.

Under the Stalinist regime, the Czechoslovak Communist Party (CPC) sought to enforce strict adherence to Soviet-style socialism and consolidate their power over all aspects of society. The key figure in this era was the Czechoslovak Communist Party leader, Klement Gottwald, who served as the President of Czechoslovakia.

The Stalinist policies implemented during this time aimed at transforming Czechoslovakia into a socialist state modeled after the Soviet Union. These policies included the collectivization of agriculture, nationalization of industries, and the suppression of political opposition. The state exerted control over all areas of society, including the economy, media, education, and cultural institutions.

Collectivization of agriculture aimed to eliminate private farms and create state-controlled collective farms. This process involved forcing farmers to give up their land and join collective units, where agricultural production was centrally planned and directed by the state. This policy often met with resistance from farmers, resulting in social and economic disruptions.

The nationalization of industries involved the transfer of private businesses, factories, and enterprises into state ownership. The state took control of major industries, including mining, manufacturing, and energy, aiming to centralize economic decision-making and achieve rapid industrialization. Private property rights were greatly restricted, and the state directed economic development according to its socialist agenda.

The Stalinist regime also enforced strict ideological conformity and suppressed political opposition. Dissent and dissenters were harshly punished, and a climate of fear permeated society. The state security apparatus, including the secret police (StB), played a significant role in suppressing any perceived threats to the regime. Political purges and show trials were conducted, resulting in the imprisonment, exile, or execution of those deemed enemies of the state.

Censorship and propaganda were pervasive during the Stalinist Era. The state-controlled media disseminated communist propaganda, promoting the ideals of socialism and glorifying the achievements of the regime. Intellectual and cultural spheres were tightly controlled, with artists, writers, and intellectuals expected to adhere to socialist realism and produce works that aligned with the regime's ideology.

The Stalinist Era in Czechoslovakia came to an end with the death of Joseph Stalin in 1953. The subsequent leadership, under Antonín Novotný, continued to maintain a repressive regime, albeit with some relaxation of policies compared to the earlier years. However, the legacy of the Stalinist era had lasting effects on Czechoslovakia, shaping political, social, and cultural dynamics for years to come.

It is important to note that the Stalinist Era in Czechoslovakia was characterized by political repression, human rights abuses, and the stifling of democratic principles. The period was marked by a pervasive atmosphere of fear and conformity, with the state exerting control over every aspect of people's lives. It was a time of significant social and political transformation, as Czechoslovakia aligned itself more closely with the Soviet Union and implemented policies reflecting the Soviet model of socialism.

Prague Spring

The Prague Spring of 1968 was a period of political liberalization and reform in Czechoslovakia under the leadership of Alexander Dubček, the First Secretary of the Communist Party of Czechoslovakia. It represented a significant departure from the oppressive policies of the previous years and aimed to introduce greater political openness, civil liberties, and economic reforms.

The Prague Spring was characterized by a spirit of optimism and a desire for change. Dubček's reformist agenda, known as "Socialism with a Human Face," sought to create a more democratic and decentralized socialist system. It called for political pluralism, freedom of speech, and the protection of civil rights. The aim was to establish a socialist society based on self-management, greater individual freedoms, and a more participatory political system.

During this period, Czechoslovakia experienced a cultural and intellectual renaissance. Artists, writers, and filmmakers enjoyed greater creative freedom, expressing critical views and exploring alternative ideas. The media played a vital role in this period, with newspapers and television programs presenting a broader range of opinions and offering more open debates.

The Prague Spring also saw the relaxation of censorship, allowing the publication of previously banned books and the emergence of alternative political groups and movements. Independent student organizations, workers' councils, and intellectual circles flourished, fostering an atmosphere of open dialogue and political engagement.

However, the reforms implemented during the Prague Spring faced resistance from conservative elements within the Czechoslovak Communist Party and other Warsaw Pact countries. The Soviet Union, concerned about the potential erosion of its influence, grew increasingly wary of the changes taking place in Czechoslovakia.

On the night of August 20-21, 1968, Warsaw Pact troops, led by the Soviet Union, invaded Czechoslovakia in a military intervention known as the Warsaw Pact Invasion. The invasion aimed to halt the liberalization process and restore strict communist control. Despite some initial acts of resistance by Czechoslovak citizens, the military presence proved overwhelming, and the Prague Spring was brought to an abrupt end.

Following the invasion, a period of normalization ensued, characterized by the restoration of hardline communist policies and the suppression of dissent. Dubček was removed from his position, and his reformist allies were replaced by more conservative leaders loyal to the Soviet Union.

The Prague Spring had a profound impact on Czechoslovak society and the broader Eastern Bloc. It revealed the limitations of reform within the Soviet-dominated socialist system and demonstrated the challenges faced by those seeking political change in a repressive regime. The events of the Prague Spring left a lasting mark on the collective memory of Czechoslovakia, symbolizing both the aspirations for freedom and the subsequent disappointment and repression.

Soviet Occupation

In 1968, a period known as the Prague Spring, Czechoslovakia underwent a period of political liberalization and reform under the leadership of Alexander Dubček. The reforms aimed to create "socialism with a human face," introducing greater political freedom, freedom of the press, and decentralization of power. However, these changes were viewed as a threat by the Soviet Union and its allies in the Warsaw Pact.

In response to the reforms, on the night of August 20-21, 1968, Soviet and Warsaw Pact troops invaded Czechoslovakia. The invasion was characterized by military force, with tanks, troops, and armed personnel carriers deployed throughout the country. The primary objective was to suppress the liberalization movement and restore control over Czechoslovakia.

The Soviet occupation marked the beginning of a period of repression and control imposed by the occupying forces. The new regime installed by the Soviets, commonly referred to as the

"Normalization" period, aimed to reverse the reforms of the Prague Spring and reinstate a strict communist regime.

During the occupation, the Soviet-backed regime cracked down on political dissent, censored the media, purged reformist officials, and implemented a policy of "normalization" that aimed to restore strict communist control over society. Many intellectuals, artists, and political activists were persecuted, imprisoned, or forced into exile.

The Soviet occupation lasted for over 20 years, until the fall of communism in 1989. Throughout this period, Czechoslovakia remained under the influence and control of the Soviet Union, with the country being a satellite state within the Eastern Bloc.

The Soviet occupation had a profound impact on Czechoslovak society. It stifled political freedoms, suppressed dissent, and limited cultural and intellectual expression. However, it also fueled a sense of resistance and opposition among the Czechoslovak people, which eventually led to the emergence of the dissident movement and the eventual overthrow of the communist regime during the Velvet Revolution in 1989.

The Soviet occupation remains a significant and complex chapter in Czechoslovak history. It represents a period of foreign control, repression, and struggle for freedom and independence. The memories and legacy of the occupation continue to shape the country's collective memory and its commitment to democracy and human rights.

Normalization Era

The Normalization Era in Czechoslovakia refers to the period of political and social repression that followed the end of the Prague Spring in 1968. It lasted from the late 1960s until the late 1980s and was characterized by the restoration of strict communist control, ideological conformity, and the suppression of dissent.

After the Soviet-led invasion of Czechoslovakia in August 1968, the hardline communist leadership, supported by the Soviet Union, reasserted its control over the country. The reforms and liberalizations of the Prague Spring were reversed, and a policy of normalization was implemented to bring Czechoslovakia back in line with the Soviet-dominated Eastern Bloc.

The Normalization Era was marked by a return to orthodox communist ideology and the imposition of strict political control. The media and cultural institutions came under state censorship, with the suppression of independent voices and the promotion of state propaganda. Dissenting intellectuals, artists, and writers faced persecution, censorship, and the loss of their livelihoods. Many were forced into exile or chose to self-censor their work to avoid persecution.

Political opposition and dissent were heavily suppressed. The Communist Party purged its ranks of those associated with the Prague Spring and replaced them with loyalists to the Soviet-backed regime. Dissident groups were monitored, infiltrated, and persecuted by the secret police. Public protests and demonstrations were suppressed, and political activism was met with repression and imprisonment.

Economically, the Normalization Era witnessed a focus on heavy industry and centralized planning, with limited economic reforms and little room for private enterprise. This resulted in stagnation, inefficiency, and economic decline, as the regime prioritized political control over economic development.

Socially, the Normalization Era was characterized by a climate of fear and mistrust. Surveillance and state control extended into all aspects of life, and individuals were encouraged to report on each other, fostering a culture of suspicion. The regime sought to instill obedience and conformity, promoting a conservative and nationalist agenda that aimed to preserve communist rule.

The Normalization Era began to unravel in the late 1980s with the rise of the Velvet Revolution, a peaceful mass protest movement calling for political and social change. The regime's grip on power weakened, and popular demands for democracy, freedom of expression, and human rights gained momentum. The Normalization Era came to an end with the collapse of communism in Czechoslovakia in 1989, marking a significant turning point in the country's history.

The Velvet Revolution

The Velvet Revolution was a non-violent revolution that took place from November 17 to December 29, 1989, in Czechoslovakia. It was a pivotal moment in the country's history and led to the overthrow of the communist regime that had been in power for over four decades.

The revolution was sparked by a series of student-led protests in Prague on November 17, 1989, to commemorate the death of a student, who was killed by the communist regime earlier that month. The protests quickly grew in size and intensity, attracting support from various segments of society who were dissatisfied with the oppressive communist regime.

The protesters demanded political reforms, freedom of speech, and the end of one-party rule. As the demonstrations spread across the country, they gained momentum and public support. The communist government, unable to contain the growing unrest, eventually capitulated to the demands of the people.

Under pressure from the protesters and international pressure, the Communist Party leadership resigned, and a transitional government was formed. Václav Havel, a prominent dissident and playwright, emerged as a leading figure in the revolution and later became the first president of post-communist Czechoslovakia.

The Velvet Revolution marked the peaceful transition from a communist regime to a democratic system in Czechoslovakia. It brought an end to decades of communist rule and ushered in a new era of political freedom, civil liberties, and economic reforms. The country experienced a wave of democratic reforms, including free elections, the restoration of political pluralism, and the establishment of a market economy.

The Velvet Revolution had a significant impact not only on Czechoslovakia but also on the wider region of Central and Eastern Europe. It served as an inspiration for other countries undergoing political transformations and contributed to the eventual collapse of the Soviet Union and the end of the Cold War.

The event is remembered for its peaceful nature and the unity of the Czechoslovak people in their pursuit of freedom and democracy. The Velvet Revolution remains an important part of Czech history and is celebrated as a symbol of the power of peaceful resistance and the triumph of human rights and democratic values.

Václav Havel

Václav Havel (1936-2011) was a Czech playwright, essayist, dissident, and politician who became one of the most prominent figures in the Czech Republic's history. Havel played a crucial role in the country's transition from communism to democracy and served as the first President of the Czech Republic.

Born on October 5, 1936, in Prague, Havel grew up in a wealthy family. Despite his privileged background, he developed a deep sense of empathy and concern for the social and political issues facing his country. Havel's writings, which included plays, essays, and political commentary, captured the frustrations and aspirations of the Czech people living under communist rule.

In the 1960s, Havel emerged as a leading dissident and a vocal critic of the communist regime. His plays, such as "The Garden Party" and "The Memorandum," used humor and satire to expose the absurdities and moral decay of the communist system. Havel's activism and his role in the human rights movement led to numerous arrests and periods of imprisonment.

Following the "Velvet Revolution" in 1989, which marked the peaceful overthrow of communism in Czechoslovakia, Havel became a central figure in the country's transition to democracy. In December 1989, he was elected President of Czechoslovakia, a position he held until the country peacefully split into the Czech Republic and Slovakia in 1993. Havel then became the first President of the newly formed Czech Republic and served two terms until 2003.

As President, Havel worked to consolidate democratic institutions, promote human rights, and foster international cooperation. He advocated for Czech Republic's integration into the European Union and NATO, solidifying its place in the broader European community. Havel was known for his moral leadership, eloquence, and commitment to civic responsibility.

Beyond his political career, Havel was also recognized as a leading intellectual and moral authority. His philosophical writings explored themes of personal freedom, responsibility, and the power of the individual to challenge oppressive systems. Havel's influential essay "The Power of the Powerless" became a manifesto for nonviolent resistance and inspired movements for change around the world.

After leaving office, Havel continued to be involved in global politics and activism. He spoke out against human rights abuses and championed democratic values worldwide. Havel received numerous awards and honors for his contributions to literature, human rights, and democracy, including the prestigious Nobel Peace Prize in 1989.

Václav Havel's legacy as a statesman, intellectual, and moral voice continues to resonate both in the Czech Republic and internationally. He remains an enduring symbol of peaceful resistance, moral courage, and the transformative power of individual action. Havel's commitment to human rights and democratic principles serves as an inspiration to generations seeking justice, freedom, and the pursuit of truth.

Post-Communist Era

The Post-Communist Era refers to the period of political, social, and economic transformation that followed the collapse of communism in Central and Eastern Europe, including Czechoslovakia. After the Velvet Revolution in 1989, Czechoslovakia embarked on a journey of democratic reforms and the transition to a market-oriented economy.

During the Post-Communist Era, Czechoslovakia underwent significant changes in its political landscape. The country transitioned from a one-party communist regime to a multi-party democratic system. Free and fair elections were held, allowing citizens to choose their leaders through democratic processes. Political pluralism emerged, with various political parties competing for power and representing diverse ideologies and interests.

Economically, the Post-Communist Era witnessed the shift from a centrally planned socialist economy to a market-based economy. State-owned enterprises were privatized, and private entrepreneurship and foreign investments were encouraged. Economic reforms aimed to establish a competitive business environment, liberalize trade, and integrate into the global economy.

The Post-Communist Era also brought social and cultural changes. Freedom of speech, press, and expression were protected, enabling the development of a vibrant civil society and independent media. Civil liberties and human rights were emphasized, allowing individuals to freely express their opinions and participate in public life. The era also saw increased cultural openness and exchange, as Czechoslovakia reconnected with the international community and embraced global influences.

Challenges and complexities accompanied the Post-Communist Era. The transition process was not without difficulties, as the country faced economic restructuring, unemployment, and social inequalities. There were debates over the pace and extent of reforms, as well as tensions between preserving traditional values and embracing Western influences. However, the Post-Communist Era marked a significant turning point in Czechoslovakia's history, setting the stage for its further development as an independent and democratic nation.

In 1993, Czechoslovakia peacefully dissolved, leading to the formation of two separate countries:

the Czech Republic and Slovakia. The Post-Communist Era continued in the Czech Republic, shaping its path towards political stability, economic prosperity, and integration into the European Union and other international institutions.

Consolidation Period

The Consolidation Period in the Czech Republic refers to the time after the initial transition from communism and the establishment of democratic institutions. This phase focused on consolidating democratic processes, strengthening the rule of law, and further developing the country's political and economic systems.

During this period, the Czech Republic made significant strides in solidifying its democratic institutions and practices. The country implemented reforms to enhance the functioning of democratic governance, including improvements in the electoral system, decentralization of power, and the protection of human rights. Political stability was sought through the establishment of stable coalitions and the peaceful transfer of power through regular elections.

Economically, the focus shifted towards ensuring sustainable economic growth and development. The Czech Republic continued its market-oriented reforms, attracting foreign direct investment, and promoting entrepreneurship. Efforts were made to enhance competitiveness, innovation, and integration into the global economy. The country became a member of the European Union in 2004, which provided further opportunities for economic cooperation and growth.

The Consolidation Period also witnessed social and cultural changes in the Czech Republic. Society became more open and diverse, embracing multiculturalism and recognizing the importance of social inclusion. Civil society organizations flourished, playing an active role in advocating for various causes and promoting civic engagement. The media landscape expanded, with a plurality of outlets offering diverse perspectives and contributing to the free flow of information.

Challenges and debates also characterized the Consolidation Period. Issues such as corruption, income inequality, and political polarization emerged as areas that required attention. The process of consolidating democratic institutions and practices proved to be an ongoing endeavor, requiring continuous efforts to ensure transparency, accountability, and citizen participation.

Overall, the Consolidation Period marked a phase of maturing democracy in the Czech Republic, where democratic values, institutions, and practices became firmly entrenched. The country demonstrated its commitment to democratic principles, rule of law, and respect for human rights. It laid the foundation for the Czech Republic's continued development as a stable and prosperous European nation.

European Integration Era

The European Integration Era in the Czech Republic began with the country's accession to the European Union (EU) in 2004. This period marked a new chapter in the country's history, as it deepened its integration into the European community and embraced the opportunities and challenges that came with EU membership.

European integration brought about significant changes in various aspects of the Czech society, economy, and governance. The country became an active participant in the decision-making processes of the EU, contributing to shaping European policies and benefiting from EU funds and programs. It fostered closer ties with neighboring countries and engaged in regional cooperation to address shared challenges and promote economic growth.

Economically, EU membership opened up new opportunities for trade, investment, and access to the single market. The Czech Republic experienced increased foreign investment, improved infrastructure, and enhanced competitiveness. The adoption of the euro currency remains a topic of discussion, with the country continuing to use the Czech koruna as its currency.

In terms of governance and legislation, the Czech Republic aligned its laws and regulations with EU standards and directives, ensuring compliance with European norms in areas such as environmental protection, consumer rights, and labor laws. The country also benefited from EU programs that supported infrastructure development, education, research, and cultural exchange.

The European Integration Era also brought changes in the social and cultural fabric of the Czech Republic. The country experienced increased mobility and exchanges among EU member states, facilitating cross-cultural interactions and promoting a sense of European identity. Citizens enjoyed greater freedom of movement, allowing them to study, work, and live in other EU countries.

Challenges during the European Integration Era included adjusting to EU regulations and policies, managing the impact of globalization, and addressing socioeconomic disparities within the country. The Czech Republic actively participated in EU decision-making processes, voicing its interests and concerns while contributing to the overall development of the European project.

The European Integration Era continues to shape the Czech Republic's trajectory as an EU member state. The country actively participates in EU initiatives, engages in negotiations on various policy areas, and contributes to the European project's development. It remains committed to the principles of democracy, rule of law, and shared European values while navigating the opportunities and complexities of European integration.

Modern Era

The Modern Era in the Czech Republic represents the period from the early 2000s to the present day, characterized by continued social, political, and economic developments in the country. This era reflects the ongoing transformation and adaptation of the Czech Republic in response to various domestic and global challenges.

In the political sphere, the Czech Republic has seen the rise of new political movements and parties, reflecting the changing dynamics of the country's electorate. Different political forces have emerged, bringing diverse perspectives and policy priorities to the forefront. Issues such as governance, corruption, social justice, and environmental sustainability have gained prominence in the public discourse.

Economically, the Czech Republic has continued its path of integration into global markets and the digital economy. The country has seen significant foreign investment, particularly in manufacturing, technology, and services sectors. Innovation and entrepreneurship have been fostered, contributing to the growth of start-ups and a vibrant business ecosystem. The Czech Republic has also been actively involved in regional economic cooperation, both within the European Union and with neighboring countries.

In the social realm, the Czech Republic has experienced societal changes driven by globalization, migration, and cultural exchange. The country has become more diverse and multicultural, with increasing interaction between different communities and the influence of global trends. Efforts have been made to address social issues, promote inclusivity, and enhance social welfare systems.

Environmental sustainability and climate change have gained greater attention in the Modern Era. The Czech Republic has been working towards reducing its carbon footprint, transitioning to renewable energy sources, and implementing sustainable practices. Environmental protection, conservation, and the promotion of green technologies have become important priorities in the country's agenda.

The Modern Era has also witnessed advancements in technology and digitalization, transforming various aspects of daily life, including communication, commerce, and public services. The Czech Republic has embraced digital innovation and sought to capitalize on the opportunities presented by emerging technologies.

Challenges in the Modern Era include addressing income inequality, enhancing social cohesion, and adapting to rapid technological advancements while preserving cultural heritage and national identity. The Czech Republic continues to navigate these challenges while seeking to ensure sustainable economic growth, social progress, and democratic governance.

The Modern Era represents a dynamic and evolving period in the Czech Republic's history, characterized by ongoing changes, adaptations, and aspirations for a prosperous and inclusive society. The country's engagement with global trends, regional cooperation, and the pursuit of innovation shape its trajectory as it strives to address contemporary challenges and seize opportunities in an interconnected world.

Czech Chronology

Chronological account of rulers and significant events in Czechoslovak history:

Around 500 BC: Celtic tribes led by Sigoves from Gaul penetrated the Hercynian lands.

12 BC: Marobud, Markomanni, and Quadi conquered Bohemia and Moravia.

After Christ:

17: War between Marobud and Hermann, prince of the Cherusci.

19: Marobud was defeated by Katvald, Prince Groth, and fled to the Roman Emperor Tiberius, who assigned Ravenna as his residence.

165-180: Marcomannic Wars.

451-500: Ancestors of the present Czech and Slovak people suddenly populated the regions of Bohemia, Moravia, and Slovakia.

563: Avars devastated Bohemia during their invasion of the Frankish Empire.

623: Samo expelled the Avars from Bohemia.

627: Samo was elected king by the Czechs, Slovaks, and other Western Slavs, establishing the first Slavic state.

630: Samo defeated the army of the Frankish king Dagobert in the Battle of Domazlice.

662: Samo's empire disintegrated.

Around 700: Krok, Libuše, and Přemysl, the ancestors of the first ruling Czech dynasty.

Around 723: Prague was founded.

Until 840 in Bohemia: The Přemyslid dynasty ruled, including Nezamysl, Mnata, Vojen, Unislav, Křesomysl, and Neklan.

Around 830: Mojmír, a brave and wise Moravian prince, converted to Christianity.

840-870: Hostivít, the last pagan Czech prince.

846: Mojmír was dethroned by the German king Louis, and his nephew Rostislav became the prince. War between Hostivít and Louis.

849: Louis was defeated by the Czechs.

863: Rostislav invited Constantine (Cyril) and Methodius to Moravia.

867: The journey of the holy brothers to Rome.

869: St. Cyril in Rome.

870: Rostislav was betrayed and handed over to the Germans, led by his nephew Svatopluk, who blinded him.

870-894: Bořivoj ruled in Bohemia, and Svatopluk became the king of Great Moravia.

873: Bořivoj and Lidmila were baptized. The first Christian church in Bohemia, dedicated to St. Clement, was built in Levý Hradec.

885: St. Methodius in Velehrad.

894-912: Spytihněv I.

907: Victory of Matfah's forces over the German and Slavic armies; the fall of the Great Moravian Empire.

912-926: Vratislav I.

926-928: Drahomíra ruled as regent.

927: St. Lidmila was strangled at Tetín.

928-935: Saint Wenceslas. Establishment of St. Vitus Cathedral in Prague Castle.

935-967: Boleslaus I.

950: German King Otto I confronted Boleslaus near Prague, and Boleslaus submitted.

955: Hungarians defeated at Augsburg and on the Czech border; Boleslaus conquered Moravia and Slovakia and added them to his realm, as well as territories along the upper Oder and Vistula rivers.

965: Doubravka married Mieszko I, who was baptized in Gniezno. Baptism of the Poles.

967-999: Boleslaus II. The Czech realm at its most extensive.

973: Establishment of the Prague Bishopric. Dětmar Sas became the first bishop. - The first male monastery, St. George's at Prague Castle.

982: Vojtěch (Adalbert) became the second bishop of Prague.

993: Boleslaus founded the first Czech male monastery in Břevnov.

995-996: Conflicts between the Slavník and Vršovci families.

997: St. Vojtěch (Adalbert) martyred.

999-1002: Boleslaus III. Territories taken away from the Czech realm that Boleslaus I and II had annexed.

1002-1003: Vratislav recognized the authority of Henry II without rights and received the Czech lands as a fief from him in Regensburg.

1004: Polish forces of Bolesław the Brave expelled from Bohemia, and Oldřich and Jaromír captured Prague.

1004-1012: Jaromír.

1012-1037: Oldřich.

1028: Bretislaus, son of Oldřich, expelled the Hungarians from Moravia and became the Moravian prince.

1032: Oldřich built the Sázava Monastery for his confessor, St. Prokop.

1038-1055: Bretislav I.

1039: Military expedition to Poland. Relics of St. Adalbert brought to Prague from Gniezno.

1040: German King Henry III's army defeated at Domažlice.

1041: Henry III defeated Bretislav, who subsequently renounced Poland.

1046: Foundation of the provostry of Boleslav.

1053: Death of St. Prokop.

1055: Introduction of the Law of Seniority, determining the succession within the Přemyslid dynasty.

1055-1061: Spytihněv II.

1061-1092: Vratislav II.

1063: Establishment of the Bishopric in Olomouc.

1074: Death of St. Adalbert, abbot of Sázava.

1075: Alliance between Vratislav II and the German King Henry IV.

1081: Liberation of the Czechs from tribute payments.

1083: Henry IV conquered Rome with the help of the Czechs.

1086: Coronation of Vratislav II as King of Bohemia in Mělník.

1092-1100: Břetislav II. - Slavic liturgy disappeared in Bohemia.

1100-1107: Bořivoj II (expelled from Bohemia by Svatopluk).

1107-1109: Svatopluk.

1108: Almost complete extermination of the Vršovice family.

1109-1117: Vladislav I (yielded to Bořivoj II).

1117-1120: Bořivoj II (again).

1120-1125: Vladislav I (again).

1125-1140: Soběslav I.

1126: Victory of the Czechs over Lothar, the German king, at Chlumec.

1140-1173: Vladislav II.

1147: Vladislav II participated in the Second Crusade.

1158: Vladislav II received the royal crown from the hands of the Holy Roman Emperor Frederick Barbarossa in Eger. The Czechs, led by the king, joined Frederick in his campaign against the Italians and distinguished themselves by their bravery, capturing the city of Milan.

1173-1179: Soběslav II.

1179-1197: Period of constant disputes over the throne and frequent changes in power among the Přemyslid dynasty.

1179-1189: Bedřich.

1189-1191: Konrád Ota.

1191: Václav II.

1192: Přemysl Otakar I.

1193-1197: Jindřich Břetislav.

1197: Vladislav III (Concordant) renounced the throne in favor of his brother Přemysl Otakar.

1197-1230: Přemysl Otakar I, the first hereditary king of Bohemia.

1204: Pope Innocent III confirmed the royal dignity in Bohemia for all eternity.

1216: Přemysl Otakar abolished the Law of Seniority and introduced the order of primogeniture within the Přemyslid dynasty.

1230-1253: Václav I (also known as King Wenceslaus).

1241: The Tatars were defeated at Olomouc by Jaroslav Divišovice.

1246: The Babenberg ducal line (Austria-Styria) became extinct.

1251: Prince Přemysl was elected Duke of Austria by the estates.

1252: Prince Přemysl married the Austrian princess Margaret and acquired Styria.

1254-1255: Crusade against the pagan Prussians; Přemysl founded Königsberg.

1260: Victory of Přemysl over Béla IV at Kressenbrunn on the Moravian field.

1269: Přemysl inherited the duchies of Krossen and Krajinské from his relative Duke Oldřich.

1276: Rudolf of Habsburg invaded Austria; Přemysl, defeated, surrendered all the newly acquired lands.

1278: Přemysl was defeated for the second time by Rudolf at Suchá Krutá on the Moravian field, betrayed by Milota of Dědice, and fell in battle.

1278-1283: Otto of Brandenburg served as regent.

1281: Famine and plague in Bohemia.

1283-1305: Václav II.

1300: Crowned as King of Poland; the first Czech groschen were minted in Kutná Hora.

1305-1306: Václav III, the last of the Přemyslid dynasty.

1305: Abdicated the Hungarian crown (vacant after the extinction of the Árpád dynasty).

1306: Assassinated in Olomouc.

1306-1307: Rudolf I of Habsburg, Duke of Austria (grandson of Rudolf of Habsburg), died while besieging Horažďovice.

1307-1310: Henry, Duke of Carinthia.

1310-1346: John of Luxembourg.

1319: Bautzen (part of Upper Lusatia) was incorporated into the Bohemian realm.

1322: Cheb was given to the Bohemian king as a fief.

1327: John undertook a campaign into Poland and brought most of Silesia under the Bohemian crown.

1328: Victorious crusade to pagan Lithuania.

1330: King John's victorious campaign in Italy.

1337: Second crusade to Lithuania.

1344: Foundation of the current form of St. Vitus Cathedral on Prague Castle (Matthias of Arras, architect). Pope Clement VI elevated the Bishopric of Prague to an archbishopric. Ernest of Pardubice became the first Czech archbishop.

1345: Third crusade to Lithuania. Prince Charles had the crown of St. Wenceslas made.

1346: Prince Charles elected King of Germany; John fell in the Battle of Crécy against the English.

1346-1378: Charles I (also known as Charles IV, Holy Roman Emperor).

1348: Charles founded Charles University, the New Town of Prague, Karlštejn Castle, and a monastery in Slavonice.

1353: Charles acquired Upper Palatinate.

1354: Charles crowned Emperor in Rome.

1364: The duchies of Świdnica, Jawor, and Lower Lusatia were incorporated into the Bohemian realm. - Ernest of Pardubice.

1373: Charles acquired Brandenburg through purchase.

1325-1400: Thomas of Štítný.

1378-1419: Wenceslaus IV.

1394: Capture of Czech nobles led by Henry of Rosenberg and taken to Austria.

1402: Master Jan Hus began preaching in the Bethlehem Chapel.

1409: By royal decree, three votes were granted to the Czech nation at Charles University in Prague.

1410: Hus was excommunicated; Wycliffe's books were burned in Prague.

1414: Hus began his journey to Constance under the protection of Emperor Sigismund.

1415: Hus was burned at the stake in Constance.

1416: Jerome of Prague was burned at the stake in Constance.

1419-1437: Sigismund.

1419: The Hussites, led by Jan Žižka of Trocnov, captured the Lesser Town of Prague.

1420: Sigismund's army gathered at Vítkov (hence called Žižkov) near Prague was defeated. - Second major defeat of royal troops at Vyšehrad.

1421: Žižka lost his second eye while capturing Rabí Castle.

1424: Žižka at Přibyslav.

1426: Great victory of the Hussites over the German crusaders at Ústí nad Labem.

1427: Victorious raids of the Hussites, led by Prokop the Great, into Austria and Silesia. Battle of Tachov.

1430: Great successful Hussite expedition to the Upper Saxony and Franconia. - Prokop before Naumburg.

1431: Victory of the Czechs at Domažlice.

1434: Battle of Lipany.

1436: Council of Jihlava, acceptance of the Compacts, Czechs reconciled with the Roman Church.

1438-1439: Albert of Austria.

1439-1451: Bohemia without a king.

1444: George of Poděbrady, the highest regent.

1452-1457: Ladislaus the Posthumous.

1458-1471: George of Poděbrady as king. - Establishment of the Unity of the Brethren.

1458: George of Poděbrady accepted Matthias Corvinus as his son-in-law and helped him ascend the Hungarian throne. - Aeneas Sylvius, later Pope Pius II, wrote a Czech chronicle in Latin.

1464: Beginning of the nobility's unity against George. George is cursed.

1467: The first printing press in Bohemia is established in Pilsen.

1467: Domestic war between the king and rebellious nobility; the crusader army is defeated at Nýrsko.

1469: Matthias of Hungary is elected as the king of Bohemia by the Catholic estates. - Royal Czech forces drive out Matthias and the Hungarians from Moravia.

1471-1516: Vladislav II (Jagiellonian).

1494: Ctibor Tovačovský of Cimburk.

1500: The first Czech legal code is issued: "Constitution of King Vladislav."

1510: Bohuslav Hasistejnský of Lobkowicz.

1514: Řehoř Hrubý of Jelení.

1516-1526: Louis (Jagiellonian).

1520: Viktorin Kornelius of Všehrd.

1521: William of Pernštejn.

Habsburg Dynasty.

1526-1564: Ferdinand I.

1547: Bloody Diet in Prague.

1564-1576: Maximilian II.

1576-1611: Rudolf II. The Golden Age of the Czech language.

1599: Daniel Adam of Veleslavín.

1611-1619: Matthias.

1618: Bohemian Revolt.

1620-1637: Ferdinand II.

1632: Albrecht von Wallenstein, Duke of Friedland and imperial commander, drives out the Saxon troops from Bohemia.

1634: Wallenstein is assassinated in Cheb.

1636: Karel ze Žerotín, a highly educated writer and patron of science and art.

1637-1657: Ferdinand III.

1648: The Swedes, under the command of Königsmark, occupied Prague Castle and Lesser Town in Prague; Peace of Westphalia, end of the Thirty Years' War.

1657-1705: Leopold I.

1671: Jan Amos Comenius in Amsterdam.

1674: Karel Škréta ze Závořic, a painter.

1705-1711: Joseph I.

1714-1740: Charles II (also known as Charles VI, Holy Roman Emperor).

1737: Count František Antonín Špork, a patron of science and art.

1740-1780: Maria Theresa. The Habsburg-Lorraine dynasty on the Bohemian throne.

1742: By the Treaty of Breslau, Silesia, excluding the regions of Teschen, Krnov, and Opava, was ceded to Frederick II.

1780-1790: Joseph II.

1790-1792: Leopold II.

1792-1835: Francis I (also known as Francis II, Holy Roman Emperor).

1835-1848: Ferdinand IV (V), the Benevolent.

Since 1848: Francis Joseph I.

In 1860, on October 20th, an imperial diploma was issued, in which His Imperial Majesty restored the free constitution.

1861: The Austro-Hungarian Compromise is reached, establishing the dual monarchy of Austria-Hungary.

1867: The Austro-Hungarian Empire is formally established, granting greater autonomy to Hungary.

1879: Founding of the Czech Social Democratic Party, a major political party advocating for workers' rights and social reform.

1908: Founding of the Union of Czechoslovak Patriots, a political organization striving for greater autonomy within the Austro-Hungarian Empire.

1914: The outbreak of World War I, with Czech soldiers fighting on various fronts.

1916: The founding of the Czechoslovak National Council, a resistance movement seeking independence from Austria-Hungary.

1917: The Pittsburgh Agreement, a declaration signed by Czech and Slovak political leaders in the United States, advocating for an independent Czechoslovak state.

1918: The establishment of Czechoslovakia as an independent state following the dissolution of the Austro-Hungarian Empire. Tomáš Garrigue

Masaryk becomes the first President of Czechoslovakia.

1920: The adoption of the Constitution of Czechoslovakia, which established Czechoslovakia as a parliamentary democracy with a multi-party system.

1929: The global economic crisis, known as the Great Depression, has a severe impact on Czechoslovakia's economy, leading to high unemployment and social unrest.

1935: The signing of the Franco-Czechoslovak Treaty, which formed a defensive alliance between Czechoslovakia and France.

1938: The Munich Agreement, a diplomatic agreement between Germany, Italy, France, and the United Kingdom, leads to the cession of the Sudetenland, a predominantly German-speaking region of Czechoslovakia, to Nazi Germany.

1939: The occupation of Czechoslovakia by Nazi Germany following the German occupation of Prague. Czechoslovakia is divided into the Protectorate of Bohemia and Moravia, which becomes a Nazi puppet state, and the Slovak Republic, a separate satellite state aligned with Germany.

1939-1945: Nazi Occupation - Following the German occupation of Czechoslovakia in 1939, the country was divided into the Protectorate of Bohemia and Moravia and the Slovak Republic.

The Czech resistance movement, led by figures such as Jan Kubiš and Jozef Gabčík, carried out acts of sabotage against the Nazi regime. The country suffered under the repressive rule of the Nazis until their defeat in 1945.

1945: Liberation and Post-War Period - Czechoslovakia was liberated by Soviet and Allied forces at the end of World War II. The country underwent a process of post-war reconstruction, and democratic elections were held in 1946, leading to the establishment of a coalition government.

1948: Communist Coup - In February 1948, a communist coup led by the Communist Party of Czechoslovakia took place, leading to the establishment of a communist regime. The country transitioned into a Soviet-backed socialist state.

1950s-1960s: Communist Era - Czechoslovakia was firmly under communist rule during this period. The government implemented central planning, collectivization of agriculture, and nationalization of industries. Dissent and political opposition were suppressed, and censorship was prevalent. The country aligned itself with the Soviet Union and became a member of the Eastern Bloc.

1968: Prague Spring - In 1968, Czechoslovakia experienced a brief period of political liberalization known as the Prague Spring. Under the leadership of Alexander Dubček, the Communist Party pursued reforms aimed at introducing greater political openness, freedom of speech, and economic decentralization. However, this period of reform was met with resistance from the Soviet Union and other Warsaw Pact countries.

August 1968: Warsaw Pact Invasion - In response to the liberalization efforts of the Prague Spring, Warsaw Pact troops, led by the Soviet Union, invaded Czechoslovakia. The invasion marked the end of the Prague Spring and the restoration of hardline communist rule. The period that followed was characterized by political repression and a return to centralized control.

1969: Gustav Husák Becomes President - Gustav Husák, a prominent figure in the Communist Party, became the General Secretary of the Communist Party of Czechoslovakia and later assumed the position of President. Under his leadership, the government pursued a policy of "Normalization," which aimed to restore strict communist control and reverse the reforms of the Prague Spring.

1970s: Suppression and Repression - The Czechoslovak government under Husák's leadership cracked down on dissent and political opposition. Many reform-minded individuals were expelled from the Communist Party, imprisoned, or forced into exile. Censorship was tightened, and surveillance on citizens increased, stifling freedom of expression and civil liberties.

1977: Charter 77 - In 1977, a group of dissidents, including playwright Václav Havel, initiated the Charter 77 movement. Charter 77 criticized the government's human rights abuses and called for adherence to international agreements on civil and political rights. The movement faced severe repression, with many of its members being persecuted and imprisoned.

1989: Velvet Revolution - In November 1989, a series of peaceful protests and demonstrations took place across Czechoslovakia. These protests, known as the Velvet Revolution, demanded political reform and the end of communist rule. The regime was unable to suppress the growing wave of dissent, and in December 1989, the Communist Party relinquished its monopoly on power.

1989: Václav Havel Becomes President - In the aftermath of the Velvet Revolution, Václav Havel, a dissident playwright and key figure in the opposition movement, became the President of Czechoslovakia. Havel played a crucial role in the transition to democracy and oversaw the country's transformation.

1989: Velvet Divorce - Following the Velvet Revolution and the end of communist rule, negotiations between Czech and Slovak leaders led to the agreement to separate Czechoslovakia into two independent countries. This peaceful separation is known as the Velvet Divorce.

1993: Formation of the Czech Republic and Slovakia - On January 1, 1993, the Czech Republic and Slovakia officially became separate countries. Czechoslovakia peacefully dissolved, and both nations embarked on their individual paths.

1990s: Transition to Democracy and Market Economy - Both the Czech Republic and Slovakia underwent significant political, social, and economic transformations. They transitioned from centrally planned economies to market-based systems, implemented democratic reforms, and sought integration into European and global institutions.

2004: Czech Republic joins the European Union - On May 1, 2004, the Czech Republic, along with several other Central and Eastern European countries, became a member of the European Union. This integration brought new opportunities for trade, investment, and political cooperation.

2007: Schengen Agreement - The Czech Republic became a part of the Schengen Area, an agreement allowing for passport-free travel and cooperation on border control among member states.

2013: Presidency of Miloš Zeman - Miloš Zeman was elected as the President of the Czech Republic in 2013, serving as the country's head of state. His presidency has been marked by various political debates and controversies.

2018: Andrej Babiš as Prime Minister - Andrej Babiš, the leader of the ANO 2011 party, became the Prime Minister of the Czech Republic in 2018. His government has focused on economic policies, including fiscal stability and measures to combat corruption.

2018: Government Formation and Elections - Following the parliamentary elections in 2017, Andrej Babiš's ANO 2011 party formed a coalition government with the Czech Social Democratic Party (ČSSD). The government faced various challenges, including protests against Babiš over allegations of conflicts of interest.

2019: Protests and Political Controversies - Large-scale protests took place across the country, with citizens expressing discontent over perceived government corruption and erosion of democratic values. The demonstrations targeted Prime Minister Babiš and his government, demanding his resignation.

2020: COVID-19 Pandemic - The COVID-19 pandemic had a significant impact on the Czech Republic, as it did globally. The government implemented various measures, including lockdowns, restrictions, and vaccination campaigns, to curb the spread of the virus and protect public health.

2021: Presidential Election - In the presidential election held in January 2023, incumbent President Miloš Zeman was re-elected for a second term, defeating his opponent Jiří Drahoš. The election reflected ongoing political divisions and debates within the country.

2022: Parliamentary Elections - In the parliamentary elections held in October 2021, the ANO 2011 party led by Andrej Babiš emerged as the largest party but fell short of an overall majority. The election results paved the way for negotiations to form a new government.

Conclusion

As the author of "Czech History" and a proud Czech, I want to express my immense pride and gratitude to all of you who have joined me on this journey. This book is not just a collection of words; it is a celebration of our shared heritage and an invitation to explore the captivating story of Czech history.

To my fellow Czechs, I want to remind you of the incredible legacy we carry. Our land, located at the very heart of Europe, holds a significant place in history. From the ancient Slavs and the visionary Libuše foreseeing the greatness of Prague to the days of the Holy Roman Empire and the intellectual brilliance of figures like Jan Hus, our contributions to European civilization are immeasurable. Let us take pride in our rich heritage and continue to cherish the traditions that define us.

And to our non-Czech readers, I want to emphasize that Czech history reaches far beyond the confines of a "Soviet Eastern European" country. We are not defined solely by our association with the Soviet era, but by a vibrant and diverse history that has shaped the very core of Europe. Our nation has witnessed the rise and fall of empires, sparked intellectual movements, and nurtured artistic and cultural achievements. By exploring Czech history, you will gain a deeper understanding of the pivotal role our nation has played in shaping the European landscape.

Together, let us embrace the truth that lies within these pages and transcend the borders that divide us. Through the triumphs and struggles, the cultural achievements,and political challenges, we can gain a deeper understanding of our identity and the values we hold dear. May "Czech History" serve as a bridge that connects us, fostering a sense of unity and appreciation for the diverse threads that make up the fabric of our nation.

I am profoundly grateful to each and every one of you for joining me on this extraordinary journey through time. May "Czech History" inspire you, educate you, and instill within you a profound sense of pride for our remarkable heritage.

Josef Václav Nikolau

Josef Václav Nikolau, born on August 8, 1838, in Týn nad Vltavou, and died on April 30, 1862, in the same place, was a multifaceted figure known for his contributions as a teacher, writer, and historian. He played a significant role in shaping Czech literature and education during the 19th century.

As a teacher, Nikolau dedicated himself to the education and intellectual development of young students. He not only imparted knowledge but also fostered a love for literature and learning among his pupils. Recognizing the importance of oratory skills, Nikolau established a school of declamation, where students could refine their public speaking abilities and cultivate the art of effective communication.

Nikolau's passion for literature extended to his own writings. He focused on producing literature specifically tailored for young readers, aiming to engage and inspire them with captivating stories and moral lessons. His literary works were widely read and cherished by Czech youth, contributing to the cultural and intellectual growth of the emerging generation.

However, Nikolau's most notable contribution was his historical writings. His book titled "Czech History in Pictures for Czechoslovak Youth in National Schools" was a groundbreaking work that sought to make history accessible and engaging for young Czechoslovak students. It provided a visual narrative of Czechoslovak history, utilizing illustrations and concise descriptions to bring the past to life. The book was well-received and became a popular educational resource in national schools, helping students develop a deeper understanding and appreciation for their national heritage.

In addition to his teaching and writing endeavors, Nikolau served as an editor for a theater almanac, further showcasing his involvement in the cultural sphere. His work involved selecting and curating theatrical pieces, promoting the arts, and contributing to the vibrant theater scene of the time.

Tragically, Josef Václav Nikolau's promising career was cut short when he passed away at the age of 23 in Týn nad Vltavou. Nonetheless, his legacy as a dedicated educator, writer, historian, and promoter of Czech literature and culture continues to resonate. His contributions to the field of education, particularly in making history accessible to young minds, left an indelible mark on the intellectual landscape of Czechoslovakia.

About the Author

Kytka Hilmarová, a Prague native and political refugee, embarked on a transformative journey at a young age when she and her parents' sought asylum in the United States in 1968. As an accomplished author, translator, and publisher, Hilmarová has left an indelible mark on the literary world, bridging the gap between Czech literature and English-speaking readers.

With over 200 books brought to life as a prolific ghostwriter and a portfolio of translating more than 100 Czech literary works into English, Hilmarová acts as a vital bridge connecting Czech literature with a global audience. Her visionary approach and unwavering commitment to preserving and promoting Czech culture, history, tradition, and literature have ensured that the legacy of Czech literary works remains alive, vibrant, and cherished for generations to come.

As the founder of Czech Revival Publishing, Hilmarová showcases the rich tapestry of Czech literary gems, fostering cultural exchange and expanding the global reach of Czech authors. Through her captivating works and translations, she invites readers to immerse themselves in the enchanting world of Czech literature, offering a glimpse into its diverse themes, profound emotions, and timeless wisdom.

Join Kytka Hilmarová on a literary journey that illuminates the treasures of Czech literature, history, and tradition. Her exceptional talent, resilience, and relentless pursuit of bridging cultures make her an indispensable figure in bringing the richness of Czech literature to English-speaking audiences, ensuring its enduring legacy for years to come.

10% of book proceeds support the preservation of Czech culture in the United States. Learn more about our efforts to safeguard and enhance Czech traditions, language, arts, and history through the following:

Czechs in America Organization (CIAO) is dedicated to fostering the appreciation, understanding, and teaching of Czech culture and history. We exist to preserve, promote, and support efforts to perpetuate the Czech culture, history, customs, and traditions in the United States. CzechAmerica.org

The Czech Museum was established with the purpose of preserving, collecting, exhibiting, researching, and interpreting a collection of artifacts and archival material related to Czech history and culture. TheCzechMuseum.org

Everything Czech is dedicated to fostering a profound understanding and appreciation of the unique and vibrant history, culture, and traditions of the Czech people. EverythingCzech.com

Made in United States
Troutdale, OR
07/14/2023

11288635R00246